Ray's Guides:

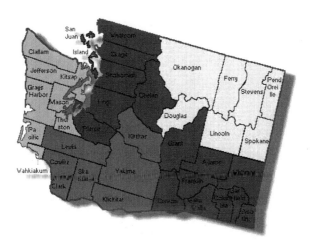

Ray Knowlton

4th Edition, Copyright January 2016 by Ray Knowlton

Ray Knowlton,   email - ray@raysguides.com

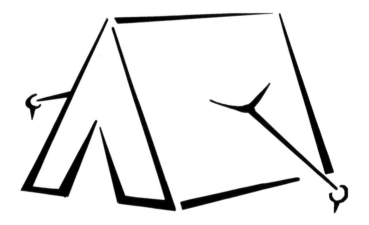

INTRODUCTION
WHY I WROTE THIS GUIDE
PASSES AND PERMITS
SAFETY AND CAMPFIRES
FISHING
HIKING
DRINKING WATER
HANDICAP ACCESSIBLE
LET'S KEEP THEM FREE

INTRODUCTION

Free Campgrounds in Washington State offers many beautiful and often remote and secluded campgrounds throughout the state. From the lush green Rainforest of the Olympic Peninsula to the rugged mountain regions of the Northeast, and south through the Yakima Valley and as far southeast as the northern reaches of the Umatilla National Forest located just south of the small but quaint town of Pomeroy.

Many others can be found from the southern border at the Columbia River northwards to the Okanogan Valley.

Rivers, streams, lakes and mountains await your visit with plenty of hiking trails available that you can use for day hike excursions or take off for days of wilderness exploring.

If you enjoy canoeing or kayaking, be sure to bring them along since many of these campgrounds are set on lakes, some big enough to spend days exploring. Bring your bicycles as well!

The most important thing though is to get out there and enjoy the beautiful areas that Washington State has to offer. Beats the heck out of camping on pavement.

Why I Wrote This Guide

I put this guide together for those of you who like me are looking for campgrounds that are smaller, more remote and secluded, which in turn makes them more private and relaxing. For those of you with kids, this is a great opportunity to get them out into a natural, more primitive wilderness setting where they can check out all the wonderful things that the great outdoors has to offer. Wilderness is great; let's pass it on.

Passes and Permits

Although all the campgrounds listed are free of charge for camping, some are located at or near trailheads. There is no fee to camp in the campground however; a Northwest Forest Pass is required for you to park your car within 1/4 mile of the trailhead. It's a good idea to pick up a pass before heading off in search of the perfect campsite. You can purchase a pass at any Forest Service Office. Prices are $5.00 for a one day pass or $30.00 for the whole year. For a list of businesses that sell the pass, call 1-800-270-7504 or look on the internet for www.naturenw.org. This pass covers all of Washington and Oregon states.

If you're over 62 or disabled, you may want to check out the Golden Age Passport or the Golden Access Passport. These are lifetime entrance passes to ALL national parks, monuments, historic sites, recreation areas and national wildlife refuges administered by the federal government which charge entrance fees. Golden Age Passports are issued to citizens or permanent residents of the United States who are 62 or older, and Golden Access Passports for the disabled. They also give you a 50 percent discount on most federal use fees charged for facilities and services such as camping, boat launching, parking, swimming sites and so on. There is a $10 onetime charge for the Golden Age Passport.

If you use the outdoors a lot, or are planning a vacation, check out the Golden Eagle Passport which is a similar pass allowing use of ALL federal recreation areas for a $65 annual fee. These special "Passports" are available at any Forest Service or National Park office.

Campgrounds that are regulated by the Department of Fish and Wildlife require a valid Washington State fishing license and recreation permit which comes free with the purchase of the fishing license. If you don't fish, you can camp at any Fish and Wildlife site using the Discover Pass.

This pass is also needed for access to all Department of Natural Resources campground and day-use sites. This pass will provide access to all Washington State Park day-use sites as well. These passes cost $10 per day or $30 for the whole year.

A Federal Dock Site Permit is required to use the docks at all up-lake sites on Lake Chelan. This includes day use. Boats not displaying a valid Federal Dock Site Permit are subject to a $50.00 fine. Federal Dock Site Permits must be displayed from May 1 to October 31. These permits may be obtained at the USDA Forest Service Ranger Station in Chelan, McGregor Outdoor Supply and the Stehekin Lodge in Stehekin, and at boat launches at 25 Mile State Park, Lake Chelan State Park and Old Bay Boat Launch in Manson. Day permits are available for $5.00 and a season permit is available for $40.00. Funds collected from the sale of the Federal Dock Site Permit are used to maintain docks and campgrounds on Lake Chelan. Permits are available at the Chelan Ranger Station.

At the end of comments is an underlined pass requirement for the site. Nothing there, no pass required. N/A at Elevation or GPS, I was unable to determine.

Safety and Campfires

The best safety measure is to use your common sense. Check the forest fire danger level before you reach for the matches. There's a reason you brought along your camp stove. Open fires sometimes just don't make sense.

Fishing

Many of the campgrounds listed in this book are set on or near lakes, rivers, creeks or the ocean, where you can fish if you want to. Don't forget to get a fishing license before you drop a line in campground lakes, rivers and creeks!

You'll have good fishing in most cases. Rainbow, cutthroat and Brown trout are abundant throughout the state with Eastern Brook trout found mostly in the Northeastern and North Central parts of the state, and along the slopes of the Cascades. Golden Trout can be found only in a few remote high country lakes where the water is cold and clear.

Some lakes offer Large and Small Mouth Bass along with Crappie and Yellow Perch. You can also take Channel Catfish. Washington's best Channel Cat fishing seems to be in the Yakima and Snake Rivers.

A Washington State fishing license is required, but kids 14 and under fish free, another reason to be sure to bring the kids along. You can purchase a fishing license at any sporting goods outlet. It wouldn't hurt to pick up the latest fishing regulations pamphlet before beginning this activity. They are available where you purchase your fishing license. Good luck!

Hiking

The hiking possibilities in Washington State are endless, with everything from short day hikes leading to beautiful alpine lakes or great vistas to

more strenuous jaunts that can last for days and take you to very remote areas that are seldom seen.
Quite a few trailheads are located at or near campgrounds that are detailed in this book. Some trailheads are signed to indicate the degree of difficulty. Don't hike alone if possible. It's not only safer to hike with a partner; it's also a lot more fun.
Know your limits and be prepared. It's not uncommon for hikers to climb into their tents on a star filled night only to wake up to a few, or more, inches of snow on the ground. At any time of the year!

Always carry the 10 essentials, even on a brief day hike.

1. Extra food
2. Extra clothing (including waterproof)
3. Map
4. Compass
5. Matches (in water proof container)
6. Fire starter
7. Knife
8. Sunglasses
9. Flashlight
10. First-aid kit.

Drinking Water

Microscopic organisms live even in the most beautiful water from springs, ponds, lakes or streams. Some of the organisms can make you sick. Don't take a chance, treat your water by boiling it for at least 5 minutes, or bring water from home. Safe drinking water supplies are only maintained at recreation sites with developed water systems. Most of the campgrounds in this book do not fall into that category.

Handicap Accessible

Many of the free campgrounds listed here are handicap accessible and some have wonderful special features, like wheelchair platforms for river viewing and barrier free interpretive trails, Handicap accessible means that the facility is connected with a barrier free route of travel from accessible parking areas. Due to topography and the primitive nature of some of these sites, routes may not be accessible to everybody with all disabilities. Campgrounds marked Handicap Accessible are not guaranteed to have restrooms specially equipped for wheelchair use. For additional resources for accessible recreation, check the Washington State website at www.ada-rec.wa.gov.

Let's KEEP Them Free

Lastly, I would like to mention something that should be of concern to each and every one of us who love not only the solitude of a quiet out-of-the-way campground, but also the great beauty that the forests and wild areas of Washington State have to offer.

Report Vandalism and Dumping

I'm sure many of you have noticed how many campgrounds have gone from free to fee over the past few years. The main reason for this is plain and simple. VANDALISM! Destroying picnic tables, bathrooms and other campground facilities, and leaving garbage behind is costing us all. And how about all of the roads, now gated, that used to be open, leading us to special fishing, picnicking or berry picking spots? The reason for these closures in most cases is because some people are using the woods as their personal dumping grounds.

Refrigerators, stoves, couches, car parts, tires and just plain trash! Do these people think this stuff is just going to dissolve in the next rain? It costs money to clean up this mess and with the budget cuts, more and more places are being closed.

What's the solution? I treat the campgrounds I visit and the nature around them with care and respect, so they'll always give you a good welcome, if you're the next camper down the road. Please do the same, and report vandalism and illegal dumping. Let's keep what we have left free and open to all of us and our kids in the future.

Pack It In - Pack It Out

I would just like to add a few of the things that we as people who care about our wilderness can do to help keep it wild. I think the most important thing is to leave your camp cleaner than when you arrived, and improved in some small way. If a fire ring has fallen apart, don't gripe, just rebuild it. If the bathroom isn't as clean as you'd like, don't gripe you know what to do. Tonight, after all, this is your home. Carry a trash bag in your vehicle. It doesn't have to be very big, just large enough to pack out your own trash and maybe a few other things that campers who were there before you left behind as litter. It only takes a minute, and if we can all do this, the forests will be happier and so will we and the next folks who make the camp their home for a night.

Photos

Pictures on campground pages do not necessarily correspond to actual site.

> *"I'd rather wake up in the middle of nowhere than in any city on earth."*
> *-- Steve McQueen*

TABLE OF CONTENTS

COASTAL REGION

NORTHWEST REGION

SOUTHWEST REGION

97. BIRD CREEK
98. ISLAND CAMP CAMPGROUND
99. KEN WILCOX HORSECAMP
100. LION ROCK
101. TEANAWAY
102. INDIAN
103. 29 PINES
104. DE ROUX
105. FISH LAKE
105. RED TOP CAMPGROUND
106. RIDERS CAMP
107. MANASTASH
108. QUARTZ MOUNTAIN
109. TAMARACK SPRINGS
110. SOUTH FORK MEADOWS
111. AHTANUM MEADOWS
111. ANTANUM CAMP AND PICNIC AREA
112. TREE PHONES
113. CLOVER FLATS
114. GREY ROCK TRAILHEAD
115. SNOW CABIN

NORTHEAST REGION

120. BOULDER CREEK/SHREW
121. LOWER BOBCAT
121. UPPER BOBCAT
122. TIFFANY SPRING
123. BEAR CREEK
124. RAMSEY CREEK
125. TWISP RIVER HORSECAMP
125. BEAVER CREEK
126. COUGAR FLATS AND LAKE
127. SPORTSMAN'S CAMP
127. ROCK CREEK
128. ROCK LAKES
128. LEADER LAKE
129. PALMER LAKE
130. CHOPAKA LAKE
131. TOATS COULEE
131. UPPER TOATS COULEE
132. COLD SPRINGS
133. UPPER COLD SPRINGS
133. NORTH FORK NINE MILE
134. LONG SWAMP
135. CRAWFISH LAKE

SOUTHEAST REGION

Coastal Region

Source: diymaps.net (c)

INCLUDES COUNTIES:

Clallam
Grays Harbor
Jefferson
Kitsap
Mason
Pacific
Thurston
Wahkiakum

COASTAL REGION

LYRE RIVER   (PORT ANGELES)

Number of sites: 11   Type: tents, small trailers
Toilets: yes   Setting: forest; river
Tables: yes   Fire: fire grates
Fishing: yes   Hiking: yes
Handicap Access: yes   Elevation: 500 feet
            GPS: Lat: 48.150087   Long: -123.832423

DIRECTIONS: [CLALLAM] From Port Angeles, travel west on Highway 117 to the junction with Highway 112 and U. S. Highway 101. Follow Highway 112 for approximately 12 miles past the town of Joyce to campground entrance on the right side of road. From there it's about .5 mile to the site.

COMMENTS: This is a beautiful campground in a forest setting located near the mouth of the Lyre River. 23 acres with a private feel to it, the campground is 15 miles from where the scenic Lyre River empties into the ocean, and provides a wheelchair access platform for river viewing and fishing. There is a group shelter. **Discover Pass**

BEAR CREEK   (PORT ANGELES)

Number of sites: 15   Type: tents, small trailers
Toilets: yes: Setting: forest; river
Tables: yes   Fire: fire grates
Fishing: yes   Hiking: yes
Handicap Access: yes   Elevation: 670 feet
            GPS: Lat: 48.070079   Long: -124.279378

DIRECTIONS: [CLALLAM] From Port Angeles, travel U. S. Highway 101 heading west toward Forks for approximately 43 miles to the campground entrance on the left side of the highway.

COMMENTS: There is an easy loop trail that follows the Sol Duc River, where the fishing can be good. This is a very relaxing place to spend the day. **Note:** The drive from Port Angeles to Bear Creek Campground takes you past beautiful Crescent Lake with lakeside picnic areas. If time permits, stop and check it out the. **Discover Pass**

LA PUSH - THIRD BEACH

Number of sites: open
Toilets: no
Tables: no
Fishing: yes
Handicap Access: no

Type: tents
Setting: beach
Fire: no fire rings
Hiking: beach hike
Elevation: sea level

GPS: Lat: 47.8906 Long: -124.5990

DIRECTIONS: [CLALLAM] From Port Angeles, travel U. S. Highway 101 heading west. At the small town of Sappho, U. S. Highway 101 starts heading south. Stay south on U. S. Highway 101 for another 9 miles or so to the junction with Highway 110. Take a right here. This will take you towards Mora. Follow Highway 110 for approximately 11 miles to a large parking area on the left side of the road, marked Third Beach. It's then a 1.6 mile walk-in to the beach.

COMMENTS: The hike down to the beach is pretty flat, through a coastal forest. It's a nice beach with lots of places to camp. Don't forget your tide book. Beachcombing and Frisbee is a couple of things to do here. If you care to escape Third Beach's frequent crowds, hike left (south) 0.5 mile toward the overland trail to admire a waterfall plunging from its heights straight into the pounding waves below.

LA PUSH - SECOND BEACH

Number of sites: open
Toilets: no
Tables: no
Fishing: yes
Handicap Access: no

Type: tents
Setting: beach
Fire: no fire rings
Hiking: beach hike
Elevation: sea level

GPS: Lat: 47.8982   Long: -124.6238

DIRECTIONS: [CLALLAM] From Port Angeles, travel U. S. Highway 101 heading west. At the small town of Sappho, U. S. Highway 101 starts heading south. Stay on U. S. Highway 101 for another 9 miles or so to the junction with Highway 110. Take a right here. This will take you toward Mora. Follow Highway 110 for approximately 12 miles to a large parking area on the left side of road, marked Second Beach.

COMMENTS: As with Third Beach, this one requires a walk-in, a short hike of about .8 miles to the beach. This is a walk through a beautiful coastal forest. Don't forget to bring a tide book. There are no facilities here except firewood. Although there are some pit toilets around, it's a good idea to bring a shovel with you. The same goes for Third Beach.

WILLOUGHBY CREEK

Number of sites: 3
Toilets: yes
Tables: yes
Fishing: yes
Handicap Access: no

Type: tents, small trailers
Setting: forest; river
Fire: fire grates
Hiking: yes
Elevation: 450 feet

GPS: Lat: 47.822304   Long: -124.197421

DIRECTIONS: [JEFFERSON] From Forks, travel 12 miles south on U. S. Highway 101 to the Upper Hoh Valley road. Take a left here and continue on another 3.5 miles to the campground on the right side of the road.

COMMENTS: 3 campsites on the Hoh River. This campground is a good alternative to the Olympic National Park and close enough that is a good base for hiking the National Park trails. **Note:** Maximum RV length 21 feet and the DNR preferred method of camping here is with self contained vehicle. **Discover Pass**

MINNIE PETERSON (FORKS)

Number of sites: 8
Toilets: yes
Tables: yes
Fishing: yes
Handicap Access: yes

Type: tents, small trailers
Setting: forest; river
Fire: fire grates
Hiking: yes
Elevation: 480 feet

GPS: Lat: 47.818415 Long: -124.174921

DIRECTIONS: [JEFFERSON] From Forks, travel 12 miles south on U. S. Highway 101 to the Upper Hoh Valley road. Take a left here and continue on another 5 miles to the campground on the left side of the road.

COMMENTS: This campground is situated across the road from the Hoh River, and is in a very pretty forested area. A short drive further up the Hoh Valley road brings you to the Hoh Visitor Center. There is a wonderful handicap accessible barrier-free trail through the rain forest that leaves from the visitor center. **Discover Pass**

COTTONWOOD (FORKS)

Number of sites: 9
Toilets: yes
Tables: yes
Fishing: yes
Handicap Access: yes

Type: tents; small trailers
Setting: forest; river
Fire: fire grates
Hiking: yes
Elevation: 350feet

GPS: Lat: 47.79904 Long: -124.265125

DIRECTIONS: [JEFFERSON] From Forks travel 13 miles south on U. S. Highway 101 and then turn right at the Oil City Road on the right side of the highway. Continue on this road for another 2 miles and bear left at the Cottonwood campground sign. Follow this gravel road another 1 mile to the campground.

COMMENTS: This campground is located in a forested area on the Hoh River. The campground has a designated handicapped camp site. There is a small boat launch. **Note:** As an added feature, if instead of taking the gravel road leading to the campground, you continue straight on the Oil City road, in a few miles you will come to a trailhead that leads to a very nice beach. **Discover Pass**

HOH OXBOW   (FORKS)

Number of sites: 8   Type: tents; small trailers
Toilets: yes   Setting: forest; river
Tables: yes   Fire: fire grates
Fishing: yes   Hiking: yes
Handicap Access: yes   Elevation: 400 feet
          GPS: Lat: 47.81147 Long: -124.2502

DIRECTIONS: [JEFFERSON] From Forks, travel 13.5 miles south on U. S. Highway 101 to the campground entrance on the left side of the highway.

COMMENTS: This campground is right off of the highway, and right on the Hoh River. It has a boat launch for small craft. This campground appears to fill up early on the weekends, especially during fishing season. **Discover Pass**

SOUTH FORK HOH   (FORKS)

Number of sites: 3   Type: tents, small trailers
Toilets: yes   Setting: forest; river
Tables: yes   Fire: fire grates
Fishing: yes   Hiking: yes
Handicap Access: no   Elevation: 700 feet
          GPS: Lat: 47.80948 Long: -123.990626

DIRECTIONS: [JEFFERSON] From Forks, travel approximately 14 miles south on U. S. Highway 101 to the Hoh Mainline Road. Take a left here and continue on another 6.5 miles to the H-1000 Road. Turn left again and proceed 7.8 miles (first mile or so paved, then gravel) to campground.

COMMENTS: This one is a real beauty, very remote and secluded. Forested and situated on the south fork Hoh River. Drive past the campground and in about 2 miles you come to a couple of trailheads. **Discover Pass**

5

COPPERMINE BOTTOM   (FORKS)

Number of sites: 10   Type: tents, small trailers
Toilets: yes   Setting: forest; river
Tables: yes   Fire: fire grates
Fishing: yes   Hiking: yes
Handicap Access: no   Elevation: 1320 feet
      GPS: Lat: 47.6544214232   **Long: -124.**191937466

DIRECTIONS: [JEFFERSON] From Forks, travel south on U. S. Highway 101 for approximately 43 miles to the Clearwater road. (Milepost 147) and take a left. Continue on this road for another 12.5 miles to the campground entrance. Turn right and follow this road 1.5 miles to the campground.

COMMENTS: This campground is primitive and secluded. There are ten sites that swing in an arc around one loop on the Clearwater River, a tributary of the Queets. Most of the secluded sites have little trails leading to the shallow, pebbly bottomed river. **Discover Pass**

UPPER CLEARWATER   (FORKS)

Number of sites: 10   Type: tents, small trailers
Toilets: yes   Setting: forest; river
Tables: yes   Fire: fire grates
Fishing: yes   Hiking: yes
Handicap Access: yes   Elevation: 900 feet
      GPS: Lat: 47.676932   Long: -124.121299

DIRECTIONS: [JEFFERSON] From Forks, travel south on U. S. Highway 101 for approximately 43 miles to the Clearwater road, Milepost 147, and take a left. Continue on this road for another 16 miles to the campground entrance on the right.

COMMENTS: This is another campground on the Clearwater River. This very remote campground doesn't appear to get a lot of use. It is peaceful and there is a hand boat launch. **Discover Pass**

6

YAHOO LAKE   (FORKS)

Number of sites: 4   Type: tents
Toilets: yes   Setting: forest; lake
Tables: yes (2)   Fire: fire grates
Fishing: yes   Hiking: yes
Handicap Access: no   Elevation: 1100 feet
GPS: Lat: 47.676564   Long: -124.018172

DIRECTIONS: [JEFFERSON] From Forks, drive south on U. S. Highway 101 for approximately 43 miles to Clearwater Road, milepost 147. Take a left here and proceed onward to the entrance of the Coppermine Bottom campground. From there, continue on Clearwater Road another .25 mile to the junction and bear right, as if heading for Upper Clearwater campground. This is now a one-lane paved road. In another 3.5 miles this turns into Forest Service Road C-3100. Continue on. In another, almost 3 miles you will come to another junction and again, bear right. The road now turns to gravel. Go another 2 miles to the gate on the left side of the road. From here, it's an easy .5-mile walk-in to the campground.

COMMENTS: Of the three campgrounds in the vicinity, this one is the most remote. There is a trail that circles the lake. It is forested, with fishing, hiking trails nearby. Even if you don't want to camp here, it's a nice place to spend the day. **Discover Pass**

A society grows great when old men plant trees whose shade they know they shall never sit in.

-- Greek Proverb

7

CAMPBELL TREE GROVE (ABERDEEN)

Number of sites: 10
Toilets: yes
Tables: yes
Fishing: yes
Handicap Access: no

Type: tents, small trailers
Setting: forest; river
Fire: fire grates
Hiking: yes
Elevation: 2000 feet

GPS: Lat: 47.4809833 Long: -123.690177

DIRECTIONS: [GRAYS HARBOR] From Aberdeen, travel approximately 34 miles north on U. S. Highway 101 to the Newbury Creek Road. (Forest Service Road 2220). Take a right here, and continue on for 9 miles until you come to a "T" in the road. Go left and proceed another 9 miles (gravel road) to campground entrance.

COMMENTS: Set in gigantic old Douglas fir trees close to the eastern boundary of Colonel Bob Wilderness. Sites are on the West Fork Humptulips River. A forest hiking trail access is here, and wilderness trail access is nearby. NWFP

CHETWOOT (ABERDEEN)

Number of sites: 8
Toilets: yes
Tables: yes
Fishing: yes
Handicap Access: no

Type: tents
Setting: forest; lake
Fire: rock fire rings
Hiking: yes
Elevation: 800 feet

GPS: Lat: 47.390194 Long: -123.605056

DIRECTIONS: [GRAYS HARBOR] From Aberdeen, travel north on U.S. Highway 101 for about 32 miles to the Donkey Creek Road. Take a right and continue 22 miles. (First part paved second part gravel). At the junction with the road to Coho Campground take a left towards Coho Camp. Follow this road to the campground boat launch and set sail, or hike in.

COMMENTS: This camp offers fishing, boating, swimming and wildlife viewing. Bring your canoe or kayak and hammock and check this place out. This is a very beautiful spot.

ELKHORN DISPERSED CAMPGROUND (BRINNON)

Number of sites: 20	Type: tents
Toilets: no	Setting: forest; river
Tables: yes	Fire: fire grates
Fishing: yes	Hiking: yes
Handicap Access: no	Elevation: 600 feet

GPS: Lat: 47.729886 Long: -123.094583

DIRECTIONS: From the small town of Brinnon, follow US Highway 101 north for just over one mile to Dosewallips River Road and take a left. Continue on this road for about 9 miles to where the road is washed out and park. From here it's about a mile hike in to the site.

COMMENTS: This, now a dispersed site, is set along the peaceful Dosewallips River in beautiful forest. There are no toilets but you'll find some tables. Because of the hike in this is a now a less used camp.

OXBOW (OLYMPIA)

Number of sites: 12	Type: tents
Toilets: yes	Setting: forest; river
Tables: yes	Fire: fire grates some sites
Fishing: yes	Hiking: yes
Handicap Access: no	Elevation: 520 feet

GPS: Lat: 47.40889 Long: -123.310833

DIRECTIONS: [MASON] From Olympia, drive north on U. S. Highway 101 for about 31 miles. At the Skokomish Valley Road, take a left. At about 5 miles, you come to a "Y", where you bear right. The road gets a little bumpy for about a mile, then turns to gravel for another 2 miles or so, and then back to pavement. Continue on this road to the campground entrance on the right side of the road.

COMMENTS: This camp offers a number of primitive dispersed campsites located near the South Fork Skokomish River; this is a good place to have your camp stove handy. The river passes both sides of the campground with nice swimming holes along with fishing and hiking in a forested area.

LENA LAKE   (OLYMPIA)

Number of sites: 28   Type: tents; small trailers
Toilets: yes   Setting: forest; lake
Tables: yes   Fire: fire grates
Fishing: yes   Hiking: yes
Handicap Access: no   Elevation: 1800 feet
GPS: Lat: 47.624167 Long: -123.165833

DIRECTIONS: [MASON] From Olympia, travel north on U.S. highway 101 for about 40 miles and take a left onto Forest Service road 25 towards Hamma Hamma. Follow this road for another 8 miles to the Lena Lakes trailhead # 810.

COMMENTS: This is a hike in campground of about 3 miles. The sites are set on a beautiful mountain lake. This is a good family hike or first time backpack adventure. Activities include hiking into The Brothers Wilderness, wildlife viewing, fishing, and swimming. **NWFP** required at trailhead.

KAMMENGA CAMPGROUND   (BELFAIR)

Number of sites: 2   Type: tents, small trailers
Toilets: yes   Setting: forest; creek
Tables: yes   Fire: fire grates
Fishing: yes   Hiking: yes
Handicap Access: no   Elevation: 330 feet
GPS: Lat: 47.41701 Long: -122.908599

DIRECTIONS: [MASON] From the small town of Belfair, go left onto Highway 300 and continue on for about 3.5 miles to the Belfair-Tahuya Road and take a right. Follow this road for another 2 miles to the Effendaul Pass Road and take another right. Following this road for less than 3 miles brings you to the Goat Ranch Road, signed Spillman Campground. Take a left here and in another .3 miles turn right onto the Kammenga Road. Continue on this road for .3 miles to the campground entrance on the right.

COMMENTS: This site is one of two in the area that are used by ORV enthusiasts. If this isn't you, you may want to find another campground. **Discover Pass**

10

CAMP SPILLMAN   (BELFAIR)

Number of sites: 8   Type: tents, small trailers
Toilets: yes   Setting: forest; river
Tables: yes   Fire: fire grates
Fishing: yes   Hiking: yes
Handicap Access: no   Elevation: 350 feet
        GPS: Lat: 47.472619   Long: -122.932012

DIRECTIONS: [MASON] From the small town of Belfair, go left onto Highway 300 and continue on for about 3.5 miles to the Belfair-Tahuya Road and take a right. Follow this road for another 2 miles to the Effendaul Pass Road and take another right. Following this road for another less than 3 miles brings you to the Goat Ranch Road, signed Spillman Campground. Take a left here and in another .5 to the site.

COMMENTS: Set close to the Tahuya River, this is another site used mainly by ORV enthusiasts. It can get noisy here as you may imagine. If you are looking for solitude, this probably isn't for you. **Discover Pass**

TUNERVILLE   (OLYMPIA)

Number of sites: 3   Type: tents
Toilets: yes   Setting: forest; creek
Tables: yes   Fire: fire grates
Fishing: yes   Hiking: yes
Handicap Access: no   Elevation: 480 feet
        GPS: Lat: 47.514342   Long: - 122.882096

DIRECTIONS: [WAHKIAKUM] From Olympia, travel south on Interstate 5 for approximately 55 miles to the Highway 4 exit heading west to Longview. Continue on Highway 4 for about 54 miles to the Salmon Creek Road and take a right. Follow this road for another 9 miles. The pavement ends after 3.5 miles and in another 5.5 miles you come to a "Y" and the junction with Road 5970. Bear left here and follow this road about a mile to the campground on your right.

COMMENTS: This small campground offers real solitude. It's located in deep forest on a stream with lots of room to roam. Activities include hiking and horseback riding. Well worth the journey. **Discover Pass**

SNAG LAKE (OLYMPIA)

Number of sites: 4
Toilets: yes
Tables: yes
Fishing: yes
Handicap Access: yes

Type: tents
Setting: forest; lake
Fire: fire grates
Hiking: yes
Elevation: 1000 feet

GPS: Lat: 46.423835   Long: -123.822085

DIRECTIONS: [WAHKIAKUM] From Olympia, travel south on Interstate 5 for approximately 55 mile to the Highway 4 exit heading west to Longview. Continue on Highway 4 for about 60 miles. At the Naselle Youth Camp Road, milepost 3, take a right and proceed up, up, up for about 3 miles to the C-2600 Road and take a left. Follow this road another .5 mile to the C-2400 Road and take a right to the campground on your right.

COMMENTS: This beautiful mountain lake is one you don't want to miss if you're in the area. Perfect for a canoe or kayak. There is hiking, horseback riding and swimming. There is also a handicap access barrier-free trail around the lake with views. **Discover Pass**

WESTERN LAKES (OLYMPIA)

Number of sites: 3
Toilets: yes
Tables: yes
Fishing: yes
Handicap Access: no

Type: tents
Setting: forest
Fire: fire grates
Hiking: yes
Elevation: 1000 feet

GPS: Lat: 46.420074   Long: -123.815737

DIRECTIONS: [WAHKIAKUM] From Olympia, travel south on Interstate 5 for approximately 55 miles to the Highway 4 exit heading west to Longview. Continue on Highway 4 about 60 miles. At the Nasselle Youth Camp road, milepost 3, take a right and proceed uphill for about 3 miles to the C-2600 Road and take a left. Continue on this road, past the 2400 Road to a "Y" and bear right on the C-line Road. Keep going short distance to the campground on your right.

COMMENTS: Another beautiful mountain lake close to Snag Lake, with wonderful scenery. This very secluded camp offers hiking, horseback riding and swimming. **Discover Pass**

PORTER CREEK   (OLYMPIA)

Number of sites: 15
Toilets: yes
Tables: yes
Fishing: yes
Handicap Access: yes

Type: tents, small trailers
Setting: forest; creek
Fire: fire grates
Hiking: yes
Elevation: 400 feet

GPS: Lat: 46.9714   Long: -123.2744

DIRECTIONS: [THURSTON] From Olympia, travel west on Highway 8 for about 15 miles to junction with Highway 12. Take Highway 12 east towards Oakville for about 5.5 miles to the Porter Creek Road and take a left. Continue on this road for another 3.5 miles to an intersection where you want to go straight onto the B-line Road, gravel, and in another .5 miles bear left at the "Y" and follow this road to the campground on your right.

COMMENTS: This campground is located in the Capitol Forest, with access to Porter Creek. Fishing, hiking, and horseback riding are options here as well as mountain biking. **Discover Pass**

NORTH CREEK   (OLYMPIA)

Number of sites: 5
Toilets: yes
Tables: yes
Fishing: yes
Handicap Access: no

Type: tents, small trailers
Setting: forest; creek
Fire: fire grates
Hiking: yes
Elevation: 375 feet

GPS: Lat: 46.8900   Long: -123.2022

DIRECTIONS: [THURSTON] From Olympia, travel west on Highway 8 for about 15 miles to junction with Highway 12. Take Highway 12 east towards Oakville for about 9.5 miles to the Capitol Forest Road and take a left. This road turns into the D-line Road. Continue on this road for 4 miles to campground on your right.

COMMENTS: A little-known, wooded campground managed by the Department of Natural Resources is set along Cedar Creek, which offers fishing. There are trails for hikers only, no horses or mountain bikes are allowed. A four-mile loop trail leads to Sherman Valley. **Discover Pass**

SHERMAN VALLEY   (OLYMPIA)

Number of sites: 7   Type: tents, small trailers
Toilets: yes   Setting: forest; creek
Tables: yes   Fire: fire grates
Fishing: yes   Hiking: yes
Handicap Access: no   Elevation: 385 feet
           GPS: Lat: 46.8956   Long: -123.1522

DIRECTIONS: [THURSTON] From Olympia, travel west on Highway 8 for about 15 miles to junction with Highway 12. Take Highway 12 east towards Oakville for about 9.5 miles to the Capitol Forest Road and take a left. This road turns into the D-line Road. Continue on this road for another 6.5 miles to the campground on your right.

COMMENTS: This is another relaxing spot situated on Porter Creek in a wooded setting. This camp is located in the Capitol Forest and run by DNR. **Discover Pass**

MIMA FALLS TRAILHEAD   (OLYMPIA)

Number of sites: 5   Type: tents, small trailers
Toilets: yes   Setting: forest
Tables: yes   Fire: fire grates
Fishing: no   Hiking: yes
Handicap Access: no   Elevation: 275 feet
           GPS: Lat: 46.9019, -123.0640

DIRECTIONS: [THURSTON] From Olympia, travel south on Interstate 5 to the Littlerock exit, exit 95. Follow this road for about 8 miles to the town of Littlerock. This road now turns into 128th Ave. and you want to keep going straight on this road for .5 miles to the Waddle Creek Road and take a left. Continue on for another mile or so to the Bordeaux Road and take a right. Follow this road for about .5 miles to the Marksman Road and go right again. Continue on for another mile or so to the campground entrance on your left.

COMMENTS: This equestrian-oriented trailhead has a horse ramp and room for horse trailers. The trailhead provides hikers, horseback riders, and mountain bikers access to Capitol State Forest non-motorized trails. **Discover Pass**

MARGARET McKENNY   (OLYMPIA)

Number of sites: 25   Type: tents, small trailers
Toilets: yes   Setting: forest; creek
Tables: yes   Fire: fire grates
Fishing: yes   Hiking: yes
Handicap Access: yes   Elevation: 290 feet
            GPS: Lat: 46.925098 Long: -123.0615317

DIRECTIONS: [THURSTON] From Olympia, travel south on Interstate 5 to the Littlerock exit, exit 95. Follow this road for about 8 miles to the town of Littlerock. This road now turns into 128th Ave. Keep going straight on this road for .5 miles to the Waddle Creek Road and take a right. Follow Waddle Creek Road for about 1.5 miles to the campground entrance on your left.

COMMENTS: This is a large campground with a stream nearby, and a campground host. Things to do include hiking and horseback riding. About .5 miles or so before you reach this site; there is a road to the left marked "Mima Mounds Natural Area". It's only about a mile to the site, and well worth the journey. There is an interpretive display and about 1900 feet of handicap access barrier-free paved trail through the mysteriously mounded prairie. **Discover Pass**

Now I see the secret of making the best person, it is to grow in the open air and to eat and sleep with the earth.

--Walt Whitman

15

MIDDLE WADDLE CREEK   (OLYMPIA)

Number of sites: 24	Type: tents, small trailers
Toilets: yes	Setting: forest; creek
Tables: yes	Fire: fire grates
Fishing: yes	Hiking: no
Handicap Access: yes	Elevation: 250 feet

GPS: Lat: 46.939   Long: -123.0779

DIRECTIONS: [THURSTON] From Olympia, travel south on Interstate 5 to the Littlerock exit, exit 95. Follow this road for about 8 miles to the town of Littlerock. This road now turns into 128th Ave. Continue straight on this road for .5 miles to the Waddle Creek road and take a right. Follow Waddle Creek Road for about 2.5 miles to the campground on your left.

COMMENTS: This wooded campground is nestled along Waddell Creek in the Capitol Forest. The trails in the immediate vicinity are used primarily for all-terrain vehicles, ATVs, making for some noise. The camp spots are paved however and there are pit toilets among the 3 loops. All sites have camp fire rings and picnic tables. Area is wooded and offers good privacy among other campsites. **Discover Pass**

FALL CREEK (OLYMPIA)

Number of sites: 6	Type: tents, small trailers
Toilets: yes	Setting: forest; creek
Tables: yes	Fire: fire grates
Fishing: yes	Hiking: yes
Handicap Access: yes	Elevation: 650 feet

GPS: Lat: 46.9428 Long: -123.1272

DIRECTIONS: [THURSTON] From Olympia, drive south on Interstate 5 to the Littlerock exit, exit 95. Follow this road for about 8 miles to the town of Littlerock. This road now turns into 128th Ave. Keep going straight on this road for .5 miles to the Waddle Creek Road and take a right. Continue on Waddle Creek Road for about 3.5 miles to a "T" and go left on Sherman Valley Road. Follow this road for another mile to junction with Noschka Road and bear left. Proceed about 2.5 miles on, now gravel road, to C-6000 and take a left. Follow this road another 2 miles to the site on your right.

COMMENTS: This campground is a little more remote than some of the others in this area. The camp is set in a mountain and forest setting, on Fall Creek. It has hiking and horseback riding trails. This is a very beautiful spot. **Discover Pass**

"The wonder is that we can see these trees and not wonder more"

- Ralph Waldo Emerson

DISPERSED CAMPGROUNDS

LOWER BIG QUILCENE TRAILHEAD

Lower Big Quilcene Trail #833 starts 6 miles southwest of Quilcene on FS Road #2700-080. The Big Quilcene Trail has two segments. This is the lower access. Take US Highway 101 south of Quilcene 1.0 mile to Penny Creek Road on the right. Follow Penny Creek Road for one mile staying left at the "Y" travel 1.5 miles of gravel road to the Forest Service boundary and paved FS Road #27. Continue on road #27 another 1.5 miles to FS Road #080. Turn left onto road #080 and drive 0.5 miles to the trailhead. You'll find small parking area with limited turn around for horse trailers, picnic table and vault toilet.

FOREST ROAD # 25

Travel US Highway 101 to FS Rd. #25 (Hamma Hamma Recreation Area) 14 miles north of Hoodsport. Turn west on FS Rd. #25 and when the road turns to gravel there is a beautiful dispersed site on the left that sets right on the Hamma Hamma River. This is a large site in the trees. Further up the road there are a few more sites that are nice but closer to the road.

SPIDER LAKE DISPERESED

From Olympia, travel north on U. S. Highway 101 for 31 miles to the Skokomish Valley Road. Take a left and continue on another 5 miles where you come to a "Y". Bear right. The road gets a little bumpy for a mile or so then turns to gravel for another 2 miles, then back to pavement. You are now on Forest Service Road 23. Continue on this road. When you come to the Oxbow campground entrance, keep going for another .5 mile to the junction with Brown Lake and Spider Lake. Bear left towards Spider Lake and continue on another 8 miles to the Spider Lake Trailhead. Once you reach the trailhead, take a left onto forest road 2350 and you will see the dispersed spot on the left. There are two sites one with a table. No toilets. There are also a couple of camp spots along the lake shore. The trail loops around Spider Lake from the trailhead on upper road through old growth forest and lush plants along trail.

SLAB CAMP/DEER RIDGE TRAILHEAD CAMP

From Sequim, travel approximately 2.5 miles west on US Highway 101 and take a left on Taylor Cutoff Road just after crossing the Dungeness River. Follow Taylor Cutoff Road to Lost Mountain Road and proceed to the intersection of Forest Service Road 2870 and turn left. Continue on Forest Service Road 2870 and take a right onto Forest Road 2875. Follow this road four miles to the trailhead. This is a three unit rustic camping area adjacent to the parking area and provides access to the Slab Camp Trail #838 and the Deer Ridge Trail #846.

WYNOOCHEE FALLS

From Aberdeen, travel approximately 32 miles north on U. S. Highway 101 to the Donkey Creek Road. Take a right and continue on another 22 miles, (first half paved, second half gravel). At the junction with Coho campground which goes left, you want to keep going straight for another .5 mile. You will then come to a "T" where you want to go left. This is Forest Service Road 22. Continue on this road for another 9 miles to the campground parking area on the left. This one requires about a .5 mile walk-in. Most all of the campsites are located in a meadow. The very pretty waterfalls make this one worth the walk-in.

Northwest Region

Includes Counties:

Chelan
Island
King
Pierce
San Juan
Skagit
Snohomish
Whatcom

TEXAS PONDS   (DARRINGTON)

Number of sites: 3	Type: tents; small trailers
Toilets: yes	Setting: forest; lake
Tables: 2	Fire: fire rings
Fishing: yes	Hiking: yes
Handicap Access: no	Elevation: 1500 feet

GPS: Lat: 48.367979   Long: -121.586063

DIRECTIONS: [SKAGIT] From the town of Darrington, travel Highway 530 towards Rockport and Highway 20 for about 6 miles and bear left at the Sauk River Christian Camp sign. Continue on this paved road for about 1.1 miles and take a left onto a gravel road. This road is at the far end of the Christian camp. Follow this road for about 2.5 miles and at the "T", you want to bear right. Keep going on this road a short distance to the camping area.

COMMENTS: Right before crossing a small bridge you'll see a spot on the left with table and rock fire ring. Cross the bridge and there is another site in the trees to the right with rock fire ring only. Then a little further up on the left is another site with table, fire grate and a toilet. This is a beautiful forested area set on Texas Ponds which is lake size. Big enough to cruise around in a kayak or bring an inner tube.

> *"The best time to plant a tree was 20 years ago. The next best time is now"*
>
> *~Chinese Proverb*

SLOAN CREEK   (DARRINGTON)

Number of sites: 4	Type: tents, small trailers
Toilets: yes	Setting: forest; creek
Tables: yes	Fire: rock fire rings
Fishing: yes	Hiking: yes
Handicap Access: yes	Elevation: 2050 feet

GPS: Lat: 48.0579168   Long: -121.2882203

DIRECTIONS: [SNOHOMISH] From Darrington, travel you want to follow the Mountain Loop Highway for about 15 miles, the road will go gravel at about the halfway mark and stay that way until you reach the Monte Cristo Trailhead, and take a left onto the Forest Service Road 49. Continue on this road for another 6.5 miles and at the "Y", bear left into the campground.

COMMENTS: This remote little campground is set on Sloan Creek with both hiking and horseback riding trails in the area. There is a horse corral at the campground. **Note:** After turning onto Forest Service Road 49, go about 1 mile and there is a trailhead on your right that leads to the North Fork Falls. It's only a .3 mile walk, and well worth it. **NWFP**

MONTE CRISTO   (DARRINGTON)

Number of Sites: 5   Type: tents
Toilets: yes   Setting: forest
Tables: yes   Fire: rock fire rings
Fishing: no   Hiking: yes
Handicap Access: no   Elevation: 2950 feet
              GPS: Lat: 48.026927   Long: -121.443853

DIRECTIONS: [SNOHOMISH] From Darrington, travel south on the Mountain Loop Highway for about 20 miles and take a left onto the Monte Cristo Road.

COMMENTS: This is a hike in or bicycle in campground. Site is set at the old Monte Cristo town site. There's lots of exploring to do here. Pack it in, pack it out. Please. **Note:** At about 1/2 mile the foot bridge crossing the river is history. There is a log crossing on a good size log. After crossing, the trail is good. At about 1 mile past the crossing you will come to Haps Camp. This is a one spot camp that will accommodate two tents. Right on the river, there is an outhouse at this site. A quarter of a mile before reaching Haps Camp there is a trail going right to a nice little dispersed camp also right on the river. **NWFP**

ASHLAND LAKES   (DARRINGTON)

Number of Sites: 6   Type: tents
Toilets: yes   Setting: forest; lake
Tables: no   Fire: rock fire rings
Fishing: yes   Hiking: yes
Handicap Access: no   Elevation: 2050 feet
              GPS: Lat: 48.0477   Long: -121.7142

DIRECTIONS: [SNOHOMISH] From Darrington, travel south on the Mountain Loop Highway for about 35 miles and take a left onto Forest Service Road 4020. Follow this road for another 1.5 miles and bear right onto Forest Service Road 4021. From here it's about 1.5 miles to the trailhead.

COMMENTS: This is a walk-in camp, with the first campground about 1.5 miles in. There are a total of 5 lakes in the area all within 5 miles of the trailhead, all following one after the other. All sites have toilets and fire grates. This is a nice area to spend some time at. **Discover Pass**

BOARDMAN LAKE HIKE-IN (DARRINGTON)

Number of Sites: 5	Type: tents
Toilets: yes	Setting: forest
Tables: no	Fire: rock fire rings
Fishing: yes	Hiking: yes
Handicap Access: no	Elevation: 2750 feet

GPS: Lat: 48.0337 Long: -121.6858

DIRECTIONS: [SNOHOMISH] From Darrington, travel south on the Mountain Loop Highway for about 35 miles and take a left onto Forest Service Road 4020. Follow this road for another 1.5 miles and stay left at the "y" continuing on road 4020 to the end of the road and the trailhead.

COMMENTS: This is a short .8 mile hike-in campground. You'll find benches and tent pads. Further up the trail you'll find a large group camp with 3 benches and tent pads. Hidden away is a backcountry toilet. A Northwest Forest Pass is required for each vehicle parked at the trailhead. **NWFP**

FRENCH CREEK (ARLINGTON)

Number of Sites: 5	Type: tents; small trailers
Toilets: yes	Setting: forest; creek
Tables: no tables	Fire: rock fire rings
Fishing: yes	Hiking: yes
Handicap Access: no	Elevation: 1100 feet

GPS: Lat: 48.25061989 Long: -121.8172555

DIRECTIONS: [SNOHOMISH] From Arlington, drive east for about 19.5 miles and just after passing the milepost 41, take a right onto Forest Service road 2010. Follow this road for about 1 mile to the camp on the left.

COMMENTS: There are 2 turnout areas on the left before you reach the vault toilet on the right side of the road. From these turnouts, it's a short walk to the campsites. The other campsites are across the road from the bathroom and a short walk up the trail to the right. The bathroom is accessible but the campsites are not. All the sites are set close the creek. **NWFP**

SCHREIBERS MEADOW   (SEDRO WOOLLEY)

Number of sites: 4   Type: tents
Toilets: yes   Setting: forest; creek
Tables: yes   Fire: fire grates
Fishing: yes   Hiking: yes
Handicap Access: yes   Elevation: 1160 feet
        GPS: Lat: 48.7070622 Long: -121.8125642

DIRECTIONS: [WHATCOM] From Sedro-Woolley, travel east on Highway 20 for about 15 miles and take a left onto the Baker Lake Road. Follow this road for 12.5 miles and turn left onto Forest Service Road 12. In about 3 miles turn right onto Forest Service Road 13. Continue on this road for 6 miles to the campground and trailhead.

COMMENTS: This campground is set at the trailhead leading to Schreibers Meadow, Railroad Grade, and the Park Butte lookout shelter. This is a very popular hike with great views of Mount Baker. **NWFP**

MAPLE GROVE   (SEDRO WOOLLEY)

Number of sites: 5   Type: tents
Toilets: yes   Setting: forest; lake
Tables: yes   Fire: fire grates
Fishing: yes   Hiking: yes
Handicap Access: no   Elevation: 1000 feet
        GPS: Lat: 48.6456 Long: -121.6746

DIRECTIONS: [WHATCOM] From Sedro Woolley, travel east on Highway 20 for about 15 miles and take a left onto the Baker Lake Road. Follow this road for about 14 miles and take a right at the Baker Lake Dam Road. Continue on down this road and take a left before going over the dam and in about a mile you'll come to the boat launch.

COMMENTS: This is a boat or hike in campground. To hike in, follow the road over the dam, staying to the left, and drive a couple of miles to the trailhead on the left. Hike about 4 miles to camp. To boat in, after launch, head up the lake to the campground which will be on your right. Watch for boat dock. This is a beautiful forested area with nearby hiking trails.

25

LOWER SANDY   (SEDRO WOOLLEY)

Number of sites: 5   Type: tents
Toilets: yes   Setting: forest; lake
Tables: no   Fire: fire grates
Fishing: yes   Hiking: yes
Handicap Access: no   Elevation: 800 feet
                 GPS: Lat: Not Available

DIRECTIONS: [WHATCOM] From Sedro Woolley, travel east on Highway 20 for about 15 miles and take a left onto the Baker Lake Road. Follow this road for about 16 miles. After passing the entrance for Horseshoe Cove campground, take the next right and follow this for about 1 mile to the site.

COMMENTS: This is a drive to or boat-in campground. The sites on the left as you enter set in the woods and the one camp on the right sets closer to the lake. All sites have lake access for fishing and swimming on a hot day.

LITTLE PARK CREEK   (SEDRO WOOLLEY)

Number of sites: 1   Type: tents; small trailers
Toilets: yes   Setting: forest; creek
Tables: no   Fire: rock fire rings
Fishing: yes   Hiking: yes
Handicap Access: no   Elevation: 800 feet
                 GPS: Lat: Not Available

DIRECTIONS: [WHATCOM] From Sedro Woolley, travel east on Highway 20 for about 15 miles and take a left onto the Baker Lake Road. Follow this road for about 18.5 miles and just before you cross the Park Creek Bridge, and before you get to the Baker Lake Resort road on the right, take a left onto an unmarked road then a quick right into the site.

COMMENTS: This one site camp sets right on Park Creek. There is an outhouse tucked back in the trees. There's room for a few tents or a small trailer. You have to be the early bird to get this one. Better come during the week.

BAKER RIVER TRAILHEAD   (SEDRO WOOLLEY)

Number of sites: 6	Type: tents
Toilets: yes	Setting: forest; river
Tables: (3)	Fire: rock fire rings
Fishing: yes	Hiking: yes
Handicap Access: yes	Elevation: 900 feet

GPS: Lat: 48.75044634   Long: -121.5552829

DIRECTIONS: [WHATCOM] From Sedro-Woolley, travel east on Highway 20 for about 15 miles and take a left onto the Baker Lake Road. Follow this road for about 25 miles. The last 7 miles are gravel, and lead to the campground and trailhead.

COMMENTS: This campground is located at the end of Baker Lake road. The campsites are set in the woods and there is camping on the sand bar near the river. The trail splits with one trail leading to Baker Lake and the other trail to Sulphide Creek. Both are easy hikes. **NWFP**

"Of all the paths you take in life, make sure a few of them are dirt"

-- (Anonymous)

LILY & LIZARD LAKES   (MOUNT VERNON)

Number of sites: 6/3
Toilets: no
Tables: no
Fishing: yes
Handicap Access: no

Type: tents
Setting: forest; lake
Fire: rock fire rings
Hiking: yes
Elevation: 1900 feet

GPS: Lat: 48.5715   Long: -122.4186

DIRECTIONS: [SKAGIT] From Mount Vernon, travel north on Interstate 5 for about 15 miles to the Alger exit # 240. Take a left and go back over the freeway and follow this road for about .5 miles to the Barrel Springs Road and take another left. Continue on this road for another mile or so and take a right onto the road signed Blanchard Mountain Trails. Follow this road around past the large parking area on the right signed for Lily and Lizard lakes and keep going another mile or so, staying right, and you'll come to another trailhead for the lakes on your left. You can park here or a bit further up in a large open area. Starting here saves you about a mile walk.

COMMENTS: This is another hike-in campground. It is about 3 miles of moderate hiking to the junction with Lizard Lake going off to the right and Lily heading off to the left. Both are about .5 miles from this point. Lizard has 3 sites, Lily 6 sites. Both beautiful and just off the new Pacific Northwest Trail that goes forever. Also in the area is a trail leading to the Oyster Dome, a popular hike with good views. **Discover Pass**

PINE & CEDAR LAKES   (MOUNT VERNON)

Number of sites: 4
Toilets: yes
Tables: no
Fishing: yes
Handicap Access: no

Type: tents
Setting: forest; lake
Fire: rock fire rings
Hiking: yes
Elevation: 1550 feet

GPS: Lat: 48.6881 Long: -122.4555

DIRECTIONS: [WHATCOM] From Bellingham, travel south on Interstate 5 for about 8 miles to the Samish Way exit # 246. Take a right, then another quick left onto the Old Samish Road. Follow this road for about 2 miles to the trailhead parking area on the left.

COMMENTS: These are both hike in camps. Although both of these lakes are close in miles, the trail starts up and stays that way for about 1.8 miles. If you make it that far, you've got it made. Both camps provide peaceful settings with many trails in the area including the Raptor Ridge Trail where if you're lucky, you may spot some Bald Eagles soaring high. **Discover Pass**

HANNEGAN PASS   (SEDRO WOOLLEY)

Number of sites: 4
Toilets: yes
Tables: yes
Fishing: yes
Handicap Access: no

Type: tents; small trailers
Setting: forest; creek
Tables: yes   Fire: fire rings
Hiking: yes
Elevation: 3100 feet

GPS: Lat: 48.910210 Long: -121.591885

DIRECTIONS: [WHATCOM] From Sedro-Woolley, travel north on Highway 9 for approximately 23 miles to a "T" and the junction with the Mount Baker Highway. Take a right and in about 8.3 miles bear right at the "Y" staying on Highway 542. Continue on for another 24 miles or so and take a left onto the Hannegan Pass Road, Forest Service Road 32. Follow this road for another 5 miles to the campground.

COMMENTS: Set on Ruth Creek, this campground features 4 private sites. The Hannegan Pass trail begins here, a 4 mile one way jaunt that eventually enters the North Cascades National Park. **NWFP**

LUMMI ISLAND   (BELLINGHAM)

Number of sites: 5   Type: tents
Toilets: yes   Setting: beach; forest
Tables: (3)   Fire: fire rings
Fishing: yes   Hiking: yes
Handicap Access: no   Elevation: 100 feet
GPS: Lat: 48.658251 Long: -122.613822

DIRECTIONS: [WHATCOM] From Bellingham, travel north on I-5 for about 6 miles and take the Lummi Island/Slater Road off ramp, exit 260. In about .3 miles take the 3rd exit from the roundabout onto Slater Road. Continue on another .2 miles and take the 1st exit from the next roundabout onto Slater Road. Follow this road another 3.5 miles and turn left onto Haxton Way. Then take the 2nd exit from the roundabout staying on Haxton Way. Continue on for about 4.5 miles and turn right on Lummi Island Ferry. Board the ferry for a short trip to Lummi Island. This is a boat only access campground set near the southeast end of the island.

COMMENTS: Lummi Island Campground, within the Lummi Island Natural Resources Conservation Area, offers views of Samish Island and Bellingham Bay. The site is maintained by the Whatcom Association of Kayak Enthusiasts.

CASCADE RIVER CAMP   (MARBLEMOUNT)

Number of sites: 1   Type: tents; small trailers
Toilets: yes   Setting: forest; creek
Tables: yes   Fire: fire rings
Fishing: yes   Hiking: yes
Handicap Access: no   Elevation: 1600 feet
                GPS: Lat: Not Available

DIRECTIONS: [SKAGIT] From the town of Marblemount, on the Cascade Highway 20, keep straight onto the Cascade River Road, over the river bridge and continue on this gravel road for about 19 miles to the site on the left side of the road. This is a small site with 1 table, fire grate and there's a vault toilet just down the road, you'll pass it on the right before you arrive at the camp.

COMMENTS: This is a small site with 1 table, fire grate and there's a vault toilet just down the road, you'll pass it on the right before you arrive at the camp. This is a good camp if you want to get an early start on hiking "Cascade Pass" which is astounding.

DIABLO / GORGE LAKE   (SEDRO WOOLLEY)

Number of sites: 6   Type: tents; small trailers
Toilets: yes   Setting: forest; lake
Tables: yes   Fire: fire rings
Fishing: yes   Hiking: yes
Handicap Access: no   Elevation: 900 feet
          GPS: Lat: 48.70547 Long: -121.175561

DIRECTIONS: [WHATCOM] From Sedro-Woolley, travel east on highway 20 for approximately 59 miles and take a left onto the Diablo Road. Follow this road for .7 miles to the campground on your right.

COMMENTS: This site is set on the rather narrow Gorge Lake and offers a boat launch. There a couple of hikes in the area, one to the dam and the other, a 3.5 mile hike that takes you over creeks and into an impressive cedar grove. Further east on Highway 20, you'll find more hiker trailheads.

DIABLO LAKE CAMPS

Number of sites: 2-4
Toilets: yes
Tables: yes
Fishing: yes
Handicap Access: no

Type: tents
Setting: forest; lake
Fire: fire rings
Hiking: yes
Elevation: 1200 feet

GPS: Lat: Not Available

DIRECTIONS: [WHATCOM] From Sedro Woolley, travel east on Highway 20 for about 62 miles to the Colonial Creek Campground on the right side of the highway. Here you can launch your canoe or kayak and proceed up the lake to any of the three camps. **Note:** See Hozomeen above.

COMMENTS: All three of these camps, Hidden Cove, Thunder Point and Buster Brown are set right on the lake. Peaceful and quiet, this is a nice place to spend some time or maybe stay before heading onto Ross Lake. Nice lake for canoes and kayaks.

"Why wilderness? Because we like the taste of freedom; because we like the smell of danger"

--Edward Abbey

HOZOMEEN (SEDRO WOOLLEY)

Number of sites: 20
Toilets: yes
Tables: yes
Fishing: yes
Handicap Access: no

Type: tents; small trailers
Setting: forest; lake
Fire: fire grates
Hiking: yes
Elevation: 1650 feet

GPS: Lat: 48.99735 Long: -121.06485

DIRECTIONS: [WHATCOM] From Sedro Woolley, travel east on Highway 20 for about 62 miles to the Colonial Creek Campground on the right side of the highway. Here you can launch your canoe or kayak and proceed the five miles to the Ross Lake Dam and there use the phone to secure a portage. There is a fee of 25 dollars. Better yet, you can travel Highway 1 just three kilometers west of Hope British Columbia, exit 168, and drive the Silver-Skagit Road for 39 miles, all gravel, to the campground. **Note:** bring your canoe or kayak!

COMMENTS: Deep in the mountains, this primitive camp sits near the US-Canadian border at the north end of Ross Lake. The Silver/Skagit Road is maintained but unpaved and often rough. The East Bank trail can be accessed from the campground. This trail covers about 30 miles in distance with side trails not far from the campground.

"What is man without the beasts? If all the beasts were gone, Man would die from a great loneliness of spirit. For whatever happens to the beasts, soon happens to man. All things are connected"

--Chief Seattle

33

ROSS LAKE CAMPGROUNDS   (SEDRO WOOLLEY)

Number of sites: 19
Toilets: yes
Tables: yes
Fishing: yes
Handicap Access: no

Type: tents
Setting: forest; lake
Fire: fire rings
Hiking: yes
Elevation: 1600 feet

GPS: Lat: Not Available

DIRECTIONS: [WHATCOM] there are 19 boats in camps set on Ross Lake. Most are very private, many with trails leaving camp. Some of the sites are set on islands. You need to ferry your canoe or kayak from Diablo Lake. For more information, contact the National Park Service in Sedro Woolley at: (360) 856-5700.

COMMENTS: This is a great experience for the whole family, especially if you own a canoe or kayak. With all of the available campsites here, you can explore the lake for days. Check it out. These camps can also be accessed through Hope British Columbia. **Note:** See Hozomeen Campground above.

> *Perhaps our grandsons, having never seen a wild river, will never miss the chance to set a canoe in singing waters...glad I shall never be young without wild country to be young in"*
>
> *~Aldo Leopold*

SOUTH NAVARRE   (CHELAN)

Number of sites: 5	Type: tents
Toilets: yes	Setting: forest
Tables: yes	Fire: fire grates
Fishing: no	Hiking: yes
Handicap Access: no	Elevation: 6475 feet

GPS: Lat: 48.1053 Long: -120.339

DIRECTIONS: [CHELAN] From Chelan, travel west on Highway 150 towards Manson and from there go another 6.7 miles and take a right at the Wapato Lake Road. Follow this road for about 2.4 miles and bear right onto the Upper Joe Creek Road. From here travel about 3 miles, where the road turns into Forest Service Road 8200 and then in another .3 miles the pavement ends. Keep going and in .8 miles bear right at the "Y" and travel a mere 26 miles to the campground. This site can also be reached by following Forest Service Road 8200 past Antilion Lake and bearing right just past section D. It's still about 26 miles and except for the last couple of miles the gravel road is in pretty good condition.

COMMENTS: 35 miles from Chelan, mostly on dirt roads, this campground is for those looking to get away from it all. This is a beautiful spot to spend some time and a great jumping off spot for further travels by foot, horseback, or mountain bike. Trails include, Safety Harbor Creek, Summer Blossom and Summit Trail that will take you into some truly remote areas. There is also a large horse corral.

> *"Something will have gone out of us as a people if we ever let the remaining wilderness be destroyed"*
>
> *~Wallace Stegner*

ANTILION

Number of sites: 5   Type: tents; small trailers
Toilets: yes   Setting: forest; lake
Tables: no   Fire: fire grates
Fishing: no   Hiking: yes
Handicap Access: no   Elevation: 2500 feet
            GPS: Lat: 47.9754 Long: -120.164

DIRECTIONS: [CHELAN] From Chelan, travel west on Highway 150 towards Manson and from there go another 6.7 miles and take a right at the Wapato Lake Road. Follow this road for about 2.4 miles and bear right onto the Upper Joe Creek Road. From here travel about 3 miles to where the road turns into Forest Service Road 8200 and then in another .3 miles the pavement ends. Keep going and in another .8 miles bear left at the "Y" and go another 2 miles to the site.

COMMENTS: A primitive open sunny area on the lake, with dispersed camping. No designated campsites, the Area is large enough for groups and small RV's. Activities include fishing, canoeing, boating using only electric motors.

"Earth provides enough to satisfy every man's need,
but not for every man's greed"

~-Mahatma Gandhi

WINDY CAMP   (CHELAN)

Number of sites: 2   Type: tents; small trailers
Toilets: yes   Setting: forest; lake
Tables: yes   Fire: fire rings
Fishing: yes   Hiking: yes
Handicap Access: no   Elevation: 5900 feet
        GPS: Lat: 47.899513   Long: -120.334582

DIRECTIONS: [CHELAN] From Chelan, travel south on Highway 97 for just a mile or so and cross over the Chelan River. Continue on for 3.8 miles and take a right going towards Lake Chelan State Park. Now on Forest Service Road 23, follow this road for 25.5 miles to Forest Service Road 5900 and take a left. Keep going until you come to a "Y" and bear left towards Romona Park. Follow this, forest road 8410, for about 15 miles to the camp.

COMMENTS: This remote campground offers two tent-only sites, picnic tables, fire rings and one toilet. Trailers not advised. Also featured is a trailhead for hikers and bikers. First Creek is nearby. This camp can be pretty lonely.

GROUSE MOUNTAIN   (CHELAN)

Number of sites: 4	Type: tents
Toilets: yes	Setting: forest
Tables: yes	Fire: fire grates
Fishing: no	Hiking: yes
Handicap Access: no	Elevation: 5300 feet

GPS: Lat: 47.987   Long: -120.313

DIRECTIONS: [CHELAN] From Chelan, travel south on Highway 97 for just a mile or so and cross the bridge over the Chelan River. Continue on for 3.8 miles and take a right going towards Lake Chelan State Park. Now on Forest Service Road 23, follow this road for 25.5 miles to Forest Service Road 5900 and take a left. Keep going until you come to a "Y" and bear right. In 2 more miles you'll come to another "Y", and bear right again and then bear left at the next little junction. Continue on for 3.2 miles and stay right at the "Y" and in .5 miles you arrive at the campground on your right.

COMMENTS: 4 tent-only campsites in a primitive camping area with a number of hiking opportunities in the vicinity including the Devils Backbone trail, Pot Peak trail and Angle Peak trail.

> *"Man shapes himself through decisions that shape his environment"*
>
> *-- Rene Dubos*

38

JUNIOR POINT   (CHELAN)

Number of sites: 4   Type: tents
Toilets: yes   Setting: forest
Tables: yes   Fire: fire grates
Fishing: No   Hiking: yes
Handicap Access: no   Elevation: 6600 feet
          GPS: Lat: 47.9943   Long: -120.399

DIRECTIONS: [CHELAN] From Chelan, travel south on Highway 97 for just a mile or so and cross the bridge over the Chelan River. Continue on for 3.8 miles and take a right going towards Lake Chelan State Park. Now on Forest Service Road 23, follow this road for 25.5 miles to Forest Service Road 5900 and take a left. Keep going on this road until you come to a "Y", and bear right. In 2 more miles you'll come to another "Y" and bear right again and then bear left at the next little junction. Continue on for 3.2 miles, and stay right at the "Y". Keep going past the Grouse Mountain campground on Forest Service Road 5900, and in another 6.5 miles take a left on Forest Service Road 115 and into the site.

COMMENTS: This campground is well off the beaten path and offers four tent-only sites, campfire rings, and picnic tables. With some of the best views you are likely to find anywhere, in all directions, bring your camera. A number of hiking trails are close by.

HANDY SPRINGS   (CHELAN)

Number of sites: 1   Type: tents
Toilets: yes   Setting: forest
Tables: yes   Fire: fire grate
Fishing: no   Hiking: yes
Handicap Access: no   Elevation: 6500 feet
             GPS: Lat: 47.9786   Long: -120.411

DIRECTIONS: [CHELAN] From Chelan travel south on Highway 97 for just a mile or so and cross the bridge over the Chelan River. Continue on for 3.8 miles and take a right going towards Lake Chelan State Park. Now on Forest Service Road 23, follow this road for 25.5 miles to Forest Service Road 5900 and take a left. Keep going on this road until you come to a "Y" and bear right. In 2 more miles you'll come to another "Y" and bear right again and then bear left at the next little junction. Continue on for 3.2 miles and bear right at the "Y". Keep going past the Grouse Mountain campground on forest service 5900 and in another 7 miles take a left onto Forest Service Road 114 marked Devil's Backbone trailhead. Follow this road for .3 miles bear left at the "Y" and in another .3 miles arrive at the campground.

COMMENTS: With only one campsite, if you are the first one here, you'll have the place to yourself. **Note:** If you take a right at the last "Y" before entering the campground and go about .3 miles you come to a beautiful meadow and wonderful views. There is also a trailhead with a trail that leads to the backcountry.

DEEP CREEK   (LEAVENWORTH)

Number of sites: 6   Type: tents
Toilets: yes   Setting: forest
Tables: yes   Fire: fire grates
Fishing: yes   Hiking: yes
Handicap Access: no   Elevation: 3700 feet
GPS: Lat: 47.8197073   Long: -120.6342304

DIRECTIONS: [CHELAN] From the Leavenworth Forest Service office, travel east for about .3 miles and take a left at the Chumstick Creek Highway. Follow this road for 14.5 miles to the town of Plain and bear right onto the Beaver Valley Road. Then just ahead you want to go straight on the road marked for Thousand Trails Campground. Follow this road for 3.7 miles to a "Y" and bear right onto Forest Service Road 6100. Continue on and in 1.5 miles arrive at the campground on your right.

COMMENTS: This wooded campground is now designated dispersed. Set at a trailhead, it is one of many free campgrounds in the vicinity.

> *"Nature is just enough; but men and women must comprehend and accept her suggestions"*
>
> *--Antoinette Brown Blackwell*

DEER CAMP   (LEAVENWORTH)

Number of sites: 3   Type: tents, small trailers
Toilets: yes   Setting: forest
Tables: no   Fire: fire grates
Fishing: no   Hiking: yes
Handicap Access: no   Elevation: 3800 feet
                  GPS: Lat: Not Available

DIRECTIONS: [CHELAN] From the Leavenworth Forest Service office, travel east for about .3 miles and take a left at the Chumstick Creek Highway. Follow this road for 14.5 miles to the town of Plain and bear right onto the Beaver Valley Road. Then just ahead you want to go straight on the road marked for Thousand Trails Campground. Follow this road for 3.7 miles to a "Y" and bear right onto Forest Service Road 6100. Continue on this road for another 1.5 miles to a "T" and take a right onto Forest Service Road 6101. Follow this road and in .7 miles bear right at the "Y". Keep going and in 1.6 miles at the junction, continue on straight then in .8 miles you arrive at the campground on both sides of the road.

COMMENTS: A very secluded little spot, you probably won't have too much company here. This, like Deep Creek, is now designated dispersed. There is a trailhead at the campground.

42

MEADOW CREEK   (LEAVENWORTH)

Number of sites: 4   Type: tents, small trailers
Toilets: yes   Setting: forest; creek
Tables: (2)   Fire: fire grates
Fishing: yes   Hiking: yes
Handicap Access: no   Elevation: 2400 feet
              GPS: Lat: 47.8682 Long: -120.693

DIRECTIONS: [CHELAN] From Leavenworth, travel west on Highway 2 for about 15 miles and take a right onto County road 207 towards Fish lake. Follow this road for about 4.3 miles and bear right towards Fish Lake. Continue on this road for about 1.2 miles and take a left onto the Meadow Creek road, Forest Service Road 62. Follow this road for 2.3 miles and take a left onto Forest Service Road 6300 and go another 2.5 miles to the campground entrance road on your right. Keep on this road for .2 miles to the site.

COMMENTS: This is a small campground surrounded by trees and set along the Chiwawa River, 6 miles from Fish Lake, What a beautiful place this is.

NAPEEQUA CROSSING   (LEAVENWORTH)

Number of sites: 3   Type: tents, small trailers
Toilets: yes   Setting: forest; creek
Tables: yes   Fire: fire grates
Fishing: yes   Hiking: yes
Handicap Access: no   Elevation: 2000 feet
              GPS: Lat: 47.921 Long: -120.896

DIRECTIONS: [CHELAN] From Leavenworth, travel west on Highway 2 for about 15 miles and take a right onto County road 207 towards Fish lake. Follow this road for about 4.3 miles and stay to the left towards Lake Wenachee State park. Follow this road for about 6 miles and bear right onto the White River road. Continue on this road for another 6 miles or so to the campground.

COMMENTS: 5 campsites are located on the White River near Glacier Peak Wilderness with Wilderness trail access nearby. Activities include hiking, fishing, and picnicking. Another beautiful forest setting, this is a very nice spot for being so close to the road.

GRASSHOPPER MEADOWS   (LEAVENWORTH)

Number of sites: 6   Type: tents
Toilets: yes   Setting: forest; river
Tables: yes   Fire: fire grates
Fishing: yes   Hiking: yes
Handicap Access: no   Elevation: 2050 feet
              GPS: Lat: 47.9405   Long: -120.926

DIRECTIONS: [CHELAN] From Leavenworth, travel west on Highway 2 for about 15 miles and take a right onto County road 207 towards Fish Lake. Follow this road for about 4.3 miles and stay to the left towards Lake Wenachee State park. Follow this road for about 6 miles and bear right onto the White River road. Continue on for another 7 miles or so cross a bridge and the pavement ends. Next you want to bear left then bear left again at the Tall Timber Ranch sign. Follow this road for about 2 miles to the campground.

COMMENTS: 6 campsites are located on the White River near Glacier Peak Wilderness. Activities include hiking, picnicking, fishing, and scenic viewing. This out of the way campground is set in a wooded area with hiking trail access at end of road at White River Falls.

> *Plans to protect air and water, wilderness and wildlife are in fact plans to protect man"*
>
> *-- Stuart Udall*

WHITE RIVER FALLS   (LEAVENWORTH)

Number of sites: 4   Type: tents
Toilets: yes   Setting: forest; river
Tables: yes   Fire: fire grates
Fishing: yes   Hiking: yes
Handicap Access: no   Elevation: 2100 feet
         GPS: Lat: 47.9527   Long: -120.94

DIRECTIONS: [CHELAN] From Leavenworth, travel west on Highway 2 for about 15 miles and take a right onto County road 207 towards Fish lake. Follow this road for about 4.3 miles and stay to the left towards Lake Wenachee State park. Follow this road for about 6 miles and bear right onto the White River road. Continue on for another 7 miles or so. Cross a bridge and the pavement ends. Next you want to bear left then bear left again at the Tall Timber Ranch sign. Follow this road for about 3 miles to the campground.

COMMENTS: 5 campsites are located near the beautiful falls, in an old large tree forest and close to the boundary of Glacier Peak Wilderness.

> *The lessons we learn from the wild become the etiquette of freedom"*
>
> *-- Gary Snyder*

RAINY CREEK

Number of sites: 10
Toilets: yes
Tables: yes
Fishing: yes
Handicap Access: yes

Type: tents, small trailers
Setting: forest; creek
Fire: fire grates
Hiking: yes
Elevation: 2000 feet

GPS: Lat: 47.8485906 Long: -120.9462550

DIRECTIONS: [CHELAN] From Leavenworth, travel west on Highway 2 for about 15 miles and take a right onto County road 207 towards Fish lake. Follow this road for about 4.3 miles and stay to the left towards Lake Wenachee State park. Follow this road for about 6 miles and at junction with the Little Wenachee road bear left. Continue on this road, which turns into Forest Service Road 65, and go another 6 miles and a left onto Forest Service Road 6700. In another .5 miles bear right onto Forest Service Road 6701 and drive .7 miles to the campground on your right.

COMMENTS: 10 campsites are set on the Little Wenatchee River northwest of Lake Wenatchee. Activities include fishing, hiking in nearby Henry M Jackson Wilderness, paddling boats on the river, and wildlife viewing. This is a good family campground with lots of shade.

THESEUS CREEK

Number of sites: 2
Toilets: yes
Tables: yes
Fishing: yes
Handicap Access: yes

Type: tents, small trailers
Setting: forest; creek
Fire: fire grates
Hiking: yes
Elevation: 2200 feet

GPS: Lat: 47.8726145 Long: -121.0178772

DIRECTIONS: [CHELAN] From Rainy Creek campground, see above, continue on another 2.4 miles to the campground on the right.

COMMENTS: This campground is set right on Forest Service Road 6701 to the one side and the Little Wenatchee River on the other side, with Theseus Creek just up the road. A few of miles up the road are a couple of trails that lead into the Henry M. Jackson Wilderness.

SODA SPRINGS (LEAVENWORTH)

Number of sites: 6
Toilets: yes
Tables: yes
Fishing: yes
Handicap Access: no

Type: tents
Setting: forest; creek
Fire: fire grates
Hiking: yes
Elevation: 2000 feet

GPS: Lat: 47.851586   Long: -120.839138

DIRECTIONS: [CHELAN] From Leavenworth, travel west on Highway 2 for about 15 miles and take a right onto County road 207 towards Fish Lake. Follow this road for about 4.3 miles and stay to the left towards Lake Wenachee State park. Follow this road for about 6 miles and at junction with the Little Wenachee road bear left. Continue on this road, which turns into forest road 65, and go another 7.5 miles to the campground entrance on your left.

COMMENTS: This campground is set deep in the woods, which means a lot of shade. Set along the Little Wenatchee River with little Soda Creek close by. There is no trailer turnaround.

LAKE CREEK (LEAVENWORTH)

Number of sites: 8
Toilets: yes
Tables: yes
Fishing: yes
Handicap Access: yes

Type: tents, small trailers
Setting: forest; creek
Fire: fire grates
Hiking: yes
Elevation: 2300   feet

GPS: Lat: 47.8755   Long: -121.013

DIRECTIONS: [CHELAN] From Leavenworth, travel west on Highway 2 for about 15 miles and take a right onto County road 207 towards Fish Lake. Follow this road for about 4.3 miles and stay to the left towards Lake Wenachee State park. Follow this road for about 6 miles and at junction with the Little Wenachee road bear left. Continue on this road, which turns into forest road 65, and go another 8 or so miles. At the "Y", stay on the pavement and continue on for another 4 miles to the campground.

COMMENTS: This forested campground is set along the Little Wenatchee River. Between Lake Wenatchee and Henry M. Jackson Wilderness with trail access at the end of road.

LITTLE WENATCHEE FORD   (LEAVENWORTH)

Number of sites: 3
Toilets: yes
Tables: yes
Fishing: yes
Handicap Access: no

Type: tents
Setting: forest; creek
Fire: fire grates
Hiking: yes
Elevation: 2900 feet

GPS: Lat: 47.917891   Long: -121.0870452

DIRECTIONS: [CHELAN] From Leavenworth, travel west on Highway 2 for about 15 miles and take a right onto County road 207 towards Fish Lake. Follow this road for about 4.3 miles and stay to the left towards Lake Wenachee State park. Follow this road for about 6 miles and at junction with the Little Wenachee road bear left. Continue on this road, which turns into forest road 65, and go another 8 or so miles. At the "Y", take the gravel road for about 2.8 miles to the campground.

COMMENTS: This little campground is set high in the mountains with 2 trails heading off in different directions. The campsites are set in the trees so you can enjoy the shade. The nearest creek is a ways off, so bring plenty of water. **Note:** The last 2.8 miles of road can be pretty rough and is not recommended for trailers.

WHITE PINE   (LEAVENWORTH)

Number of sites: 5
Toilets: yes
Tables: yes
Fishing: No
Handicap Access: no

Type: tents, small trailers
Setting: forest; creek
Fire: fire grates
Hiking: yes
Elevation: 2300 feet

GPS: Lat: 47.789272   Long: -120.868645

DIRECTIONS: [CHELAN] From Leavenworth, travel west on Highway 2 for 22.5 miles and take a left on the White Pine Cascade Meadow Road. Follow this road down to the campground.

COMMENTS: This is a good little known spot. It's not far from the highway for extra convenience, but it is surprisingly very quiet. With Nason Creek nearby, there is hiking and horse riding on trails.

LAKE CHELAN BOAT-IN CAMPS:

All of the following campgrounds require a Federal Dock Site Permit.
(See passes and Permits Section)

MITCHELL CREEK   (CHELAN)

Number of sites: 7
Toilets: yes
Tables: yes
Fishing: yes
Handicap Access: no

Type: tents
Setting: forest; lake
Fire: fire grates
Hiking: yes
Elevation: 1140 feet

GPS: Lat: 47.9703 Long: -120.192

DIRECTIONS: [CHELAN] 16 miles from Chelan on the North shore.

COMMENTS: New dock with capacity for about 17 boats. This is a popular picnic area.

DEER POINT   (CHELAN)

Number of sites: 5
Toilets: yes
Tables: yes
Fishing: yes
Handicap Access: no

Type: tents
Setting: forest; lake
Fire: fire grate
Hiking: yes
Elevation: 1140 feet

GPS: Lat: 48.0266 Long: -120.313

DIRECTIONS: [CHELAN] 23 miles from Chelan on the North shore.

COMMENTS: There is 1 floating dock with capacity for about 8 boats. Good shelter from down lake wind, but no protection from up lake wind.

SAFETY HARBOR   (CHELAN)

Number of sites: 4   Type: tents
Toilets: yes   Setting: forest; lake
Tables: yes   Fire: fire grate
Fishing: yes   Hiking: yes
Handicap Access: no   Elevation: 1140 feet
          GPS: Lat: 48.0481   Long: -120.378

DIRECTIONS: [CHELAN] 26 miles from Chelan on the North shore.

COMMENTS: Floating dock accessible year round with capacity for about 6 boats. Good shelter from both up lake and down lake winds.

PRINCE CREEK   (CHELAN)

Number of sites: 6   Type: tents
Toilets: yes   Setting: forest; lake
Tables: yes   Fire: fire grates
Fishing: yes   Hiking: yes
Handicap Access: no   Elevation: 1140 feet
          GPS: Lat: 48.1469   Long: -120.496

DIRECTIONS: [CHELAN] 36 miles from Chelan on the North shore.

COMMENTS: Floating dock with capacity for about 3 boats.

MOORE POINT   (CHELAN)

Number of sites: 4   Type: tents
Toilets: yes   Setting: forest; lake
Tables: yes   Fire: fire grate
Fishing: yes   Hiking: yes
Handicap Access: no   Elevation: 1140 feet
          GPS: Lat: 48.2356   Long: -120.616

DIRECTIONS: [CHELAN] 44 miles from Chelan on the North shore.

COMMENTS: Fixed dock with capacity for about 3 boats. 1 shelter.

CORRAL CREEK   (CHELAN)

Number of sites: 4   Type: tents
Toilets: yes   Setting: forest; lake
Tables: yes   Fire: fire grate
Fishing: yes   Hiking: yes
Handicap Access: no   Elevation: 1140 feet
            GPS: Lat: 48.0464   Long: -120.444

DIRECTIONS: [CHELAN] 29 miles from Chelan on the South shore.

COMMENTS: One fixed dock with the capacity for about 4 boats.

GRAHAM HARBOR   (CHELAN)

Number of sites: 5   Type: tents
Toilets: yes   Setting: forest; lake
Tables: yes   Fire: fire grate
Fishing: yes   Hiking: yes
Handicap Access: no   Elevation: 1140 feet
            GPS: Lat: 48.0818   Long: -120.489

DIRECTIONS: [CHELAN] 32 miles from Chelan on the South shore.

COMMENTS: 1 floating dock with capacity for about 10 boats. Good shelter from down lake wind, but no protection from up lake wind.

DOMKE FALLS   (CHELAN)

Number of sites: 4   Type: tents
Toilets: yes   Setting: forest; lake
Tables: yes   Fire: fire grate
Fishing: yes   Hiking: yes
Handicap Access: no   Elevation: 1140 feet
            GPS: Lat: 48.1642   Long: -120.544

DIRECTIONS: [CHELAN] 38 miles from Chelan on the south shore.

COMMENTS: 1 floating dock with the capacity for about 6 boats.

REFRIGERATOR HARBOR   (CHELAN)

Number of sites: 4   Type: tents
Toilets: yes   Setting: forest; lake
Tables: yes   Fire: fire grate
Fishing: yes   Hiking: yes
Handicap Access: no   Elevation: 1140 feet
           GPS: Lat: 48.199321   Long: -120.587392

DIRECTIONS: [CHELAN] 41 miles from Chelan on the South shore.

COMMENTS: Accessible year around with capacity for about 4 boats.
Good down lake wind protection, but no protection from up lake winds.

DISPERSED CAMPS

DEPRESSION LAKE

From Sedro-Woolley, travel east on Highway 20 for about 15 miles and take a left onto the Baker Lake Road. Follow this road for 14 miles and take a right at the Baker Lake Dam Road. This road is new so you want to follow it and when you get to the "T" take a left and go another .3 miles or so and turn left onto an unsigned road and continue on a short distance to the lake. Depression Lake camping area is set right on the lake. Fishing and canoeing are options. If you continue on across the dam, the road leads to the Maple Grove and Watson and Anderson Lakes trailheads.

SANDY CREEK DISPERSED

From Sedro-Woolley, travel east on Highway 20 for about 15 miles and take a left onto the Baker Lake Road. Follow this road for 17 miles and take a right. (If you pass Panorama Point campground, you've gone too far). Walk down this now gated road for about .5 miles where the road ends. From here you can follow the path straight to the sites. There are a couple at paths end, but if you keep on around to the left you'll find some great camp sites right on the lake. You'll have to carry your gear about 100 yards. You can also boat in to this site.

PARK CREEK DISPERSED

About 100 yards before arriving at the Little Park Creek Camp, see page 26, take a right at an unmarked gravel road and down about 150 yards is a nice little dispersed site with a rock fire ring.

BAKER LAKE ROAD DISPERSED

From Sedro Woolley, travel east on Highway 20 for about 15 miles and take a left onto the Baker Lake Road. Follow this road for about 19 miles where the pavement ends. In another .5 miles starts a series of dispersed sites on the right side of the road. Most sites you park on the road above the sites and carry your gear down.

SHANNON CREEK DISPERSED

From Sedro Woolley, travel east on State Highway 20 for about 15 miles and take left onto the Baker Lake Rd. Continue on for about 23 miles and go left onto Forest Service Rd. 1152, which is across from the Shannon Creek Campground. Continue on road 1152 for about .5 miles and take a left onto a gravel road. A short distance down this road is a dispersed site with a rock fire ring and set on a small creek. This site looks to be more suitable for a camper van or truck with a camper although a tent would work.

CASKEY LAKE

From the town of Darrington, travel Highway 530 towards Rockport and Highway 20. In about 10.6 miles take a left onto the Concrete Sauk Valley Road. This road comes up quick so heads up. Cross over the one lane bridge and then take a left onto the Old Concrete Sauk Valley Road. Continue on this road for about 1.4 miles and take a right. Follow this road for a short distance and take the first left. Continue on this road and take the first right down a small dirt road. At the "Y" bear left into the site. This is basically a one site camp. There's a rock fire ring and a nice patch of grass for a tent. No toilets or table. Camp sets right on Caskey Lake with fishing and swimming for your enjoyment. There are some other sites in the area but not on the lake. Please pack out your trash.

FOREST RD. 49 TO SLOAN CREEK

From Darrington, you want to follow the Mountain Loop Highway for about 15 miles; the road will go gravel at about the halfway mark, and take a left onto the Forest Service Road 49. If you continue on forest road 49 towards the Sloan Creek Camp, at the "Y" instead going left into the camp, bear right and in a short distance you'll come to a large open dispersed site in the woods and close to the water.

BARLOW PASS DISPERSED

From Darrington, follow the Mountain Loop Highway for about 8 miles to Barlow Pass Scenic Drive. The road goes to gravel at this point. Continue on this road for about 9 miles where you'll come to a series of dispersed sites mostly on the riverside but a few on the high side of the road. These sites get a lot of use during the summer months and it can get dusty. Spring and fall are good times to camp here.

Just before arriving at the Monte Cristo Trailhead, there is a large dispersed site on the left side of the road. This is a good sized site and close to the water. You have to carry your gear down into the camp.

DEER CREEK TRAILHEAD CAMP

From the Verlot Public Service Center (11 miles east of Granite Falls), drive the Mountain Loop Highway for 12.5 miles and just before arriving at the Deer Creek Trailhead you'll see a couple of pullouts on the right side of the road and you can park there. There are 2 nice riverside sites and another back off in the trees. Can also be reached from Darrington following the Mountain Loop Highway. All 3 of these sites have rock fire rings but no tables. There's an outhouse toilet just up the road on the left at the trailhead.

BECKLER CREEK

After passing the Beckler River Campground, there are a series of dispersed sites on either side of the road including one with a porta-potty toilet that's on the left side of the road at about where the pavement ends. Except for this site all the others have rock fire rings only. This is a very beautiful area.

RAPID RIVER

When you come to the end of pavement, from the Beckler Creek directions above, you want to take a right onto Forest Service Road 6530. There is one single site maybe 2 miles in on the right. You have to park and then carry your gear about 100 yards, but for the privacy and beauty of the site it's worth it. A little further along 6530 at mile 3 are 3 or 4 bigger sites on the right that seemed good for groups. Pretty simple, just rock fire rings, wide open space and a clean honey bucket for all the sites. The second site in has access to a part of the river you could swim in too. Another mile or so up the road is a trail head with great hiking.

Following the Beckler River Road past the Rapid River Road, Forest Service Road 6530, take a right onto Forest Service Rd. 6550. There are 2 creek side sites on the right side of the road then crossing a bridge you'll fine 4 other dispersed sites on the left. These are pretty nice size camps with rock fire rings only.

At the junction with Forest Service Roads 65 and 63, continue on 65 towards Troublesome creek and San Juan fee campgrounds. There are a few nice dispersed sites on the left side of the road and on the creek.

Southwest Region

Includes Counties:

Clark
Cowlitz
Kittitas
Klickitat
Lewis
Skamania
Yakima

SOUTHWEST REGION

EVANS CREEK   (BUCKLEY)

Number of sites: 18
Toilets: yes
Tables: yes
Fishing: yes
Handicap Access: no

Type: tents, small trailers
Setting: forest; creek
Fire: fire grates
Hiking: yes
Elevation: 2000 feet

GPS: Lat: 46.9397368 Long: -121.937499

DIRECTIONS: [PIERCE] From Buckley, travel south on Highway 165 for about 2 miles to the junction with Highway 162 and bear left staying on Highway 165. Follow this road for about 5.5 miles and bear right at the "Y". Continue on for 8 miles and take a left into the Evan Creek trailhead. Continue on through the parking area following the road down to the site.

COMMENTS: This campground is set on Evans Creek with lots of room to roam. It has beautiful trees and lots of shade. Hiking, horseback riding and bike trails. This is an ORV area and open to 2 and 4-wheeled motorized vehicles, dirt bikes, ATVs, bicycles, etc. **NWFP**

"How is it that one match can start a forest fire, but it takes a whole box of matches to start a campfire?"

~Christy Whitehead

BUCK CREEK

Number of sites: 15	Type: tents
Toilets: yes	Setting: forest; creek
Tables: no	Fire: fire grates
Fishing: yes	Hiking: yes
Handicap Access: no	Elevation: 2650 feet

GPS: Lat: 47.01290130   Long: -121.53399658

DIRECTIONS: [PIERCE] From Enumclaw, travel east on Highway 410 for approximately 17.5 miles to the town of Greenwater. Continue on Highway 410 for another 11 miles to the Buck Creek Road and take a right. Follow this road over the bridge and in .3 miles take a left, then another quick left into the camping area on your left in the trees.

COMMENTS: There are no tables at this site, but that's not the strange thing. If you look to the right as you enter, you will see an airstrip that is still used for emergency landings. There are many campsites back in the trees. Stay clear of the airstrip. **Note:** after you cross the bridge and before you take your left, go straight for .1 mile and turn left into another camping area. This one is in dense forest. There is a vault toilet and fire rings. No tables.

> *"To cherish what remains of the Earth and to foster its renewal is our only legitimate hope of survival"*
>
> *--- Wendell Berry*

LONESOME LAKE   (ENUMCLAW)

Number of sites: 4   Type: tents
Toilets: yes   Setting: forest; lake
Tables: no   Fire: fire grates
Fishing: yes   Hiking: yes
Handicap Access: no   Elevation: 4550 feet
           GPS: Lat: 47.007987   Long: -121.66361

DIRECTIONS: [PIERCE] From Enumclaw, travel east on Highway 410 for approximately 25 miles and turn right onto Forest Service Road 74. Follow this road and in about .5 miles, bear right at the "Y". Continue on for 5.9 miles and then bear left onto Forest Service Road 7500. In another .3 miles or so, bear left again, staying on Forest Service Road 7500. Keep going, and in 3.2 miles bear right at the "Y" onto Forest Service Road 7530. Follow this road for 2.9 miles, then bear left, and continue on for .8 miles to the campground.

COMMENTS: This very remote campground is set on Lonesome Lake. There are trails in the area and fishing at the lake and in surrounding creeks. This site offers both solitude and beauty. **NWFP**

CORRAL PASS   (ENUMCLAW)

Number of sites: 20   Type: tents
Toilets: yes   Setting: forest; mountain
Tables: yes   Fire: fire grates
Fishing: no   Hiking: yes
Handicap Access: no   Elevation: 5700 feet
         GPS: Lat: 47.0105322401   Long: -121.466234456

DIRECTIONS: [PIERCE] From Enumclaw, travel east on Highway 410 for approximately 30 miles and take a left onto Forest Service Road 7174. Follow this road and in .8 miles bear left at the "Y". Continue on for another 5.2 miles to the campground.

COMMENTS: This campground is set way up high with beautiful meadows. There are many trails in the area with some offering even more spectacular views than those from camp. **Note:** the first couple of miles of road coming in are the worst so if you can get past that, you have it made. The road is not recommended for trailers.

HALF CAMP   (ENUMCLAW)

Number of sites: 4   Type: tents, small trailers
Toilets: yes   Setting: forest
Tables: no   Fire: rock fire rings
Fishing: no   Hiking: yes
Handicap Access: no   Elevation: 3600 feet
          GPS: Lat: 46.993719 Long: -121.532006

DIRECTIONS: [PIERCE] From Enumclaw, travel east on Highway 410 for approximately 34 miles and turn left onto the Crystal Mountain Road. Follow this road for 3.7 miles and take a left onto Forest Service Road 7176, then .2 miles to the site.

COMMENTS: This camp is set just outside of the Rainier National Park. If you head back down Crystal Mountain Road and go left, you will enter the Park and all of its wonders.

SAND FLAT   (ENUMCLAW)

Number of sites: 5   Type: tents, small trailers
Toilets: yes   Setting: forest; creek
Tables: no   Fire: fire grates
Fishing: yes   Hiking: no
Handicap Access: no   Elevation: 3500 feet
          GPS: Lat: 46.970004 Long: -121.496172

DIRECTIONS: [PIERCE] From Enumclaw, travel east on Highway 410 for approximately 34 miles and turn left onto the Crystal Mountain Road. Follow this road for 4.6 miles to the campground on the right.

COMMENTS: This campground is set on Silver Creek in a large open area. There are trails for both hikers and horseback riders that lead to the high country.

MILK POND CAMP   (NATCHES)

Number of sites: 3   Type: tents
Toilets: yes   Setting: forest; pond
Tables: yes   Fire: fire rings
Fishing: yes   Hiking: yes
Handicap Access: no   Elevation: 2560 feet
          GPS: Lat: 46.9872   Long: -121.063

DIRECTIONS: [KITTITAS] From Natches, travel west on Highway 12 to the junction with Highway 410 and take Highway 410 for approximately 25 miles to Forest Service Road 1708 and take a right. Follow this road for 1.3 miles to a "Y" and bear right. Continue on for .5 miles to the camping area on your right.

COMMENTS: This is only one of three free campgrounds I could find in the area. This camp sits on a little hill in the trees overlooking Milk Pond. It's a quiet little spot.

SAHARA HORSE CAMP   (ELBE)

Number of sites: 18   Type: tents, small trailers
Toilets: yes   Setting: forest
Tables: yes   Fire: fire grates
Fishing: no   Hiking: yes
Handicap Access: yes   Elevation: 1300 feet
       GPS: Lat: 46.759010580   Long: -122.08559948

DIRECTIONS: [THURSTON] From Elbe, start at the junction with Highways 706 and 7 and travel east on 706 towards Mt. Rainier for about 5 miles and take a left into the campground.

COMMENTS: This is another great family campground. There is a lot of grass, beautiful sites, and a large picnic and day use area. This camp has horseshoe pits, lots of shade and hiking and horseback riding trails nearby. **Discover Pass**

GREEN RIVER HORSE CAMP   (RANDLE)

Number of sites: 8
Toilets: yes
Tables: yes
Fishing: yes
Handicap Access: yes

Type: tents, small trailers
Setting: forest; river
Fire: fire grates
Hiking: yes
Elevation: 2865 feet

GPS: Lat: 46.349288   Long: -122.083592

DIRECTIONS: [LEWIS] From Randle, travel Forest Service Road 25 for about 10 miles, cross over the river and proceed onto Forest Service Road 26. Follow forest road 26 for about 9 miles to forest road 2612. Stay on this road for another 2 miles and take a left onto forest road 027 and into camp.

COMMENTS: 8 designated campsites, each with high lines, are limited to 2 trailer rigs or 3 vehicles. Stock water needs to be carried by bucket from the Green River until stock water facilities are completed. Several hiking and horse riding trails are accessed from the campground.

> *"The earth is not a mechanism but an organism, a being with its own life and its own reasons, where the support and sustenance of the human animal is incidental"*
>
> *-- Edward Abbey*

CODY HORSE CAMP   (RANDLE)

Number of sites: 16   Type: tents, trailers
Toilets: yes   Setting: forest; river
Tables: yes   Fire: fire grates
Fishing: yes   Hiking: yes
Handicap Access: yes   Elevation: 3100 feet
           GPS: Lat: 46.36471   Long: -121.5626

DIRECTIONS: [LEWIS] From Randle head south (across river) bare left in about one mile and follow Forest Service Road 23 for 18 miles to Forest Service Road 21, bare left onto Forest Service Road 21 and follow this road for about 4 miles to Forest Service Road 56. Turn right, pass Adams Fork Camp ground, road crosses the Cispus River and turns to gravel. Stay on Forest Service Road 56 about 3 miles to turn off to Orr Creek Snow park and Keenes Horse camp (don't turn here), then 1.7 miles further on Forest Service Road 56. You'll come to a small road to the right (Forest Service Road 054), don't turn here, then cross the Muddy Fork Creek and turn right on Forest Service Road 059. Follow this road for 1/4 mile and turn left on Forest Service Road 060. You're there.

COMMENTS: 16 pull-thru campsites are located in a forested area. Each site has a high line, table and fire ring and accommodates large trailers and trucks. There is a mounting assist ramp and stock water trough. Several hiking and horse riding trails are accessed from this area including the Pacific Crest Trail. Set in the woods this camp offers an accessible toilet and campsite The pull thru units allow for large truck and trailer rigs to 35 feet.

CHAMBERS LAKE   (PACKWOOD)

Number of sites: 8   Type: tents, small trailers
Toilets: yes   Setting: forest; lake
Tables: no   Fire: fire grates
Fishing: yes   Hiking: yes
Handicap Access: no   Elevation: 4440 feet
            GPS: Lat: 46.467894   Long: -121.537306

DIRECTIONS: [LEWIS] From Packwood, travel west on Highway 12 for about 2.5 miles to Forest Service Road 21 and take a left. Follow this road for 13 miles to Forest Service Road 2150 and turn left. Continue on this road for 3 miles to a "Y" and bear left. Keep going another .5 miles to the campground.

COMMENTS: This is another great little hideaway. The site is situated in a wooded area on little Chambers Lake. This is another great place for a canoe as well as for fishing and hiking.

CAT CREEK CHIMNEY   (PACKWOOD)

Number of sites: 5   Type: tents, small trailers
Toilets: yes   Setting: forest; creek
Tables: no   Fire: rock fire rings
Fishing: yes   Hiking: yes
Handicap Access: no   Elevation: 2900 feet
            GPS: Lat: 46.353886   Long: -121.618485

DIRECTIONS: [LEWIS] From Packwood, travel west on Highway 12 for about 2.5 miles to Forest Service Road 21 and take a left. Follow this road for about 21.5 miles to the campground on the right.

COMMENTS: This campground offers a hiking trail leaving the site. It's forested with lots of shade. **Note:** if you are coming from the town of Randle, follow Forest Service Road 23 for about 24.5 miles then bear left onto Forest Service Road 21 and go another 7 miles or so to the campground. You will pass Cat Creek Campground on the right going this way.

CAT CREEK   (PACKWOOD)

Number of sites: 5   Type: tents
Toilets: yes   Setting: forest; creek
Tables: yes   Fire: fire grates
Fishing: yes   Hiking: yes
Handicap Access: no   Elevation: 3000 feet
             GPS: Lat: 46.34854 Long: -121.623636

DIRECTIONS: [LEWIS] From Packwood, travel west on Highway 12 for about 2.5 miles to Forest Service Road 21 and take a left. Follow this road for approximately 22 miles to the campground on your left.

COMMENTS: This small campground is set on the Cispus River which can be a real mover. There are 5 back-in sites in a forest setting. The fishing and hiking opportunities in this area should keep you busy.

SUMMIT CREEK   (PACKWOOD)

Number of sites: 6   Type: tents
Toilets: yes   Setting: forest; creek
Tables: yes   Fire: fire grates
Fishing: yes   Hiking: yes
Handicap Access: no   Elevation: 2400 feet
             GPS: Lat: 46.71039 Long: -121.536754

DIRECTIONS: [LEWIS] From Packwood, travel east on Highway 12 for about 9 miles to Forest Service Road 45 and take a left. In another .3 miles you'll come to a junction and you want to go left onto Forest Service Road 4510. Follow this road for about 2 miles and take a left into Summit Creek campground.

COMMENTS: This campground is a small, rustic site located on a small flat between Summit Creek and Forest Road 4510 in a mid-elevation stand of Douglas fir, western hemlock, and western red cedar. Access to the creek is available but a high steep bank makes it challenging. The site is visually exposed to local traffic on Forest Road 4510 and can be dusty at times. The area is open with no screening between camp units.
NWFP

SODA SPRINGS (PACKWOOD)

Number of sites: 6	Type: tents, small trailers
Toilets: yes	Setting: forest; creek
Tables: yes	Fire: fire grates
Fishing: no	Hiking: no
Handicap Access: no	Elevation: 3200 feet

GPS: Lat: 46.712737   Long: -121.489584

DIRECTIONS: [LEWIS] From Packwood, travel east on Highway 12 for about 9 miles to Forest Service Road 45 and take a left. In another .3 miles you'll come to a junction and you want to go left onto Forest Service Road 4510. Follow this road for about 2 miles and at the "Y", bear left over the bridge. Continue on and in 2.5 miles you'll come to another "Y" and this time bear right onto Forest Service Road 052. In another .2 miles bear left and follow this road .3 miles to the campground.

COMMENTS: This campground is set on Summit Creek and is very remote. It's surrounded by mountains in the deep forest. You should be able to find solitude here. The Campground has 6 sites suitable for tent camping, pickup campers, or smaller trailers. Summit Creek is nearby but not visible from the site but there are a number of dispersed sites along the creek in the area. Sites have moderate screening and are not crowded. The Cowlitz Trail #44 trailhead is located in the campground, providing access to the adjacent William O. Douglas Wilderness. **NWFP**

> *"Only when the last tree has died and the last river has been poisoned and the last fish has been caught will we realize that we cannot eat money"*
>
> *-19th century Cree Indian saying*

ROCK CREEK (VANCOUVER)

Number of sites: 19   Type: tents, small trailers
Toilets: yes   Setting: forest; creek
Tables: yes   Fire: fire grates
Fishing: yes   Hiking: yes
Handicap Access: yes   Elevation: 960 feet
        GPS: Lat: 45.7640038   Long: -122.3242595

DIRECTIONS: [CLARK] From Vancouver, travel north on Interstate 5 for about 5 miles to exit 9 and go left at the bottom of the ramp. Then, at the first stop light take another left onto Highway 502 heading towards Battleground. Follow this road and in just under 2 miles take a right still going towards Battleground, still on Highway 502 east. Continue on and in 5.5 miles take a left onto Highway 503 going north. Follow this road for another 5.5 miles to the Rock Creek Road and take a right. Keep going and in about 2.5 miles, the road turns into the San Lucia Falls Road. Continue on for about 11 miles and take a right at the Sunset Falls Road. Follow this road another 2 miles to the Dole Valley Road and go right again. In about 4 miles the pavement ends and a mile further you come to the campground entrance on your left.

COMMENTS: A large campground with sites in both the shade and sun with hiking and horseback riding trails. Located on nearly 20 acres of forested land in the Yacolt Burn State Forest, there is a creek, with nice sized campsites. Campground includes, picnic tables, shelter, and vault toilets. **Discover Pass**

> *"Nature knows no difference between weeds and flowers"*
>
> *-- Mason Cooley*

COLD CREEK   (VANCOUVER)

Number of sites: 8
Toilets: yes
Tables: yes
Fishing: yes
Handicap Access: yes

Type: tents, small trailers
Setting: forest; creek
Fire: fire grates
Hiking: yes
Elevation: 1050 feet

GPS: Lat: Not Available

DIRECTIONS: [CLARK] You can follow the directions to Rock Campground Creek, above. Continue past Rock Creek entrance for 0.3 mi., keep right and go another 0.5 mi., site entrance is to right. Keep left on entrance road approximately 0.5 mi to site.

COMMENTS: Cold Creek Campground has a nice day-use area and provides access to 35 miles of the Yacolt Burn non-motorized trail system. Secluded with creek access, facilities include eight campsites, picnic tables, shelter, and a vault toilet. **Discover Pass**

CANYON CREEK   (VANCOUVER)

Number of sites: 8   Type: tents, small trailers
Toilets: yes   Setting: forest; creek
Tables: yes   Fire: fire grates
Fishing: yes   Hiking: yes
Handicap Access: no   Elevation: 1150 feet
          GPS: Lat: 45.915919   Long: -122.201638

DIRECTIONS: [SKAMANIA] From Vancouver, travel north on Interstate 5 for about 5 miles to exit 9. At the bottom of the off ramp, take a left, then, at the first stop light, take another left onto Highway 502 heading towards Battleground. Follow this road for just under 2 miles and take a right still on Highway 502 towards Battleground. Continue on for about 5.5 miles and take a left onto Highway 503 East. Keep going on this road for about 12.5 miles to the Chelatchie Road and take a right. Follow this road for another 4 miles to the Canyon Creek Road, at the Texaco station, and take another right. Continue on for about 22 miles. This road turns into Forest Service Road 54. When you come to a "Y" with Forest Service Road 54 going left and Forest Service Road 3701 going right, you want to go to the right onto 3701, and then stay left to the campground

COMMENTS: This is a great little place, well hidden with 9 small campsites in a secluded forested area near Canyon Creek. A quiet area where you can try your luck fishing in the creek. **NWFP**

MERRILL LAKE

Number of sites: 12
Toilets: yes
Tables: yes
Fishing: yes
Handicap Access: yes

Type: tents, small trailers
Setting: forest; lake
Fire: fire grates
Hiking: yes
Elevation: 1650 feet

GPS: Lat: 46.0945544   Long: -122.3120425

DIRECTIONS: [COWLITZ] From Vancouver, travel north on Interstate 5 for about 25 miles to the Woodland exit, exit 21, and take a right at the bottom of the off ramp onto Highway 503 east. Continue on for about 24 miles to junction with Highway 503 South. Stay straight on Highway 503 heading towards Cougar for another 5.5 miles and turn left at sign on highway marked Lake Merrill. This is Forest Service Road 8100. In another 4.5 miles you come to a "Y" and you want to bear left into the campground.

COMMENTS: This is tent camping only. You must walk-in, carrying your camping gear a very short distance to the sites. Situated on beautiful Merrill Lake, it is a perfect place for a canoe, or kayak. This camp offers lots of shade. There is a designated handicap access campsite available.
Discover Pass

> *The old Lakota was wise. He knew that man's heart away from nature becomes hard; he knew that lack of respect for growing, living things soon led to lack of respect for humans, too"*
>
> *~ Luther Bear*

CLIMBERS BIVOUAC   (VANCOUVER)

Number of sites: 12   Type: tents, small trailers
Toilets: yes   Setting: forest; mountain
Tables: no   Fire: rock fire rings
Fishing: no   Hiking: yes
Handicap Access: no   Elevation: 3700 feet
         GPS: Lat: 46.146695   Long: -122.181703

DIRECTIONS: [SKAMANIA] From Vancouver, travel north on Interstate 5 for about 25 miles to the Woodland exit, 21, and take a right at the bottom of the off ramp onto Highway 503 East. Continue on for about 24 miles to junction with Highway 503 South. Stay straight on 503 heading towards Cougar for another 13 miles and take a left on Forest Service Road 83. Continue on this road for 3 miles and take another left onto Forest Service Road 8100. Follow this road for 1.8 miles and bear right onto Forest Service Road 830, which is gravel. In another 2.5 miles or so you arrive at the Climbers Bivouac camping area.

COMMENTS: This camping area is located at the base of Mount St. Helens, with fantastic views. This is a hiker's paradise. Don't forget to stop at the Ape Caves on the way up.

> *"What is the use of a house if you haven't got a tolerable planet to put it on?"*
>
> *~Henry David Thoreau*

72

DOUGAN CREEK   (VANCOUVER)

Number of sites: 7
Toilets: yes
Tables: yes
Fishing: yes
Handicap Access: yes

Type: tents, small trailers
Setting: forest; creek
Fire: fire grates
Hiking: yes
Elevation: 670 feet

GPS: Lat: 45.67359   Long-122.15602

DIRECTIONS: [SKAMANIA] From Vancouver, WA, travel east on Highway 14 for about 16 miles to the town of Washougal and take a left off the highway at 15th street. Go straight on 15th Street which will soon turn into 17th Street and then into the Washougal River Road as it bends around to the right at about the 1.5 mile mark. Follow this road to its end, just past the 17 mile marker, and bear left. Continue on .5 miles to the campground entrance on the left.

COMMENTS: This very pretty campground is set in a shady forested area on Dougan Creek. There is a day use picnic area nearby and a nice viewing area of the Washougal River and the waterfalls.
Discover Pass

FALLS CREEK   (VANCOUVER)

Number of sites: 4
Toilets: yes
Tables: yes
Fishing: yes
Handicap Access: no

Type: tents, small trailers
Setting: forest; creek
Fire: fire grates
Hiking: yes
Elevation: 3500 feet

GPS: Lat: 45.966512 Long: -121.844681

DIRECTIONS: [SKAMANIA] From Vancouver, travel east on Highway 14 for about 48 miles and take a left on to the Wind River Road. Continue for about 7.8 miles to Old State Road, not the first Old State Road you come to but, the second one, it's a loop. Take a right here and then a quick left onto Panther Creek Road. In about .8 miles you come to a junction and you want to go straight. This turns into Forest Service Road 65. Follow this road for 7 miles where you will come to the four corners junction and you want to stay straight on Forest Service Road 65. Continue on and in 2 more miles, when you come to a "Y", bear right. Follow this road for 3.1 miles to the campground on your left.

COMMENTS: 4 campsites are located near the western boundary of Indian Heavens Wilderness. Several hiking or horse riding trails are in the area, including the Pacific Crest Trail. Stock loading ramps available.

"Thanks to the interstate highway system, it is now possible to travel across the country from coast to coast without seeing anything"

~Charles Kuralt, On the Road

CREST HORSE CAMP

Number of sites: 5
Toilets: yes
Tables: yes
Fishing: no
Handicap Access: no

Type: tents, small trailers
Setting: forest
Fire: fire grates
Hiking: yes
Elevation: 3500 feet

GPS: Lat: 45.9068   Long: -121.8069

DIRECTIONS: [SKAMANIA]   From Vancouver, travel east on highway 14 for about 48 miles and take a left onto the Wind River Road. Continue on for about 7.8 miles to the Old State Road. (Not the first Old State Road, but the second one. It's a loop.), and take a right, then a quick left onto the Panther Creek Road. In .8 miles, you come to a junction and you want to go straight. This turns into Forest Service Road 65. Follow this road for 7 miles where you will come to the four corners junction. You want to go right onto Forest Service Road 60 towards Crest and Trout Lake. Continue on for about 2 miles and come to a "Y" and bear right. Follow this road for .5 miles to campground.

COMMENTS: 5 primitive campsites near the Pacific Crest Trail and south of Indian Heavens Wilderness. Also has access to Big Lava Bed. Stock loading ramps are available. Hiking and horse riding on the trail.

GOVERNMENT MINERAL SPRINGS   (VANCOUVER)

Number of sites: 5
Toilets: yes
Tables: yes
Fishing: yes
Handicap Access: no

Type: tents, small trailers
Setting: forest; creek
Fire: fire grates
Hiking: yes
Elevation: 1230 feet

GPS: Lat: 45.88417   Long: -121.99583

DIRECTIONS: [SKAMANIA] From Vancouver, travel east on Highway 14 for about 48 miles and take a left onto the Wind River Road. Continue on this road for about 15 miles where it ends at the Government Springs campground. **Note:** just before arriving at the campground, Wind River Road bears off to the right. You want to stay straight.

COMMENTS: This 5 campsites in this small forested campground at the edge of Trapper Creek Wilderness. Activities include hiking the wilderness trail or fishing the creek, or fishing the Wind River nearby. Scenic driving in the area. **NWFP**

STINSON FLAT CAMPGROUND   (VANCOUVER)

Number of sites: 15
Toilets: yes
Tables: no
Fishing: yes
Handicap Access: yes

Type: tents; small trailers
Setting: river; forest
Fire: fire rings
Hiking: yes
Elevation: 600 feet

GPS: Lat: 45.92424272   Long: -121.1102023

DIRECTIONS: [KLICKITAT] From Vancouver, follow Highway 14 East along the Columbia River to the small town of Lyle. This drive is about 75 miles. At Lyle, take a left onto State Route 142. Continue on this road for about 17 miles and bear left onto the Glenwood-Goldendale Road. Continue on this road for another 9 miles and take a left at the sign for Stinson Flat Campground. Follow this gravel road down another .5 miles or so to the site.

COMMENTS: This camp features at least 15 sites in a beautiful treed area with rock fire rings, a handicap accessible toilet and boat ramp. No tables. Half a dozen sites set close to the river with the others back in the trees but all spread out nicely for privacy. There is shade here for those warm summer days. **Note:** This campground can also be reached from Goldendale by traveling west on State Route 142 for about 11 miles and bearing right onto the Goldendale-Glenwood Highway then 9 miles to the site entrance. **Discover Pass**

LEIDL BRIDGE CAMPGROUND   (VANCOUVER)

Number of sites: 35
Toilets: yes
Tables: (2)
Fishing: yes
Handicap Access: no

Type: tents; small trailers
Setting: river; forest
Fire: fire rings
Hiking: yes
Elevation: 650 feet

GPS: Lat: 45.93694277   Long: -121.1187269

DIRECTIONS: [KLICKITAT] From Vancouver, follow Highway 14 East along the Columbia River to the small town of Lyle. This drive is about 75 miles. At Lyle, take a left onto State Route 142. Continue on this road for about 17 miles and bear left onto the Glenwood-Goldendale Road. Continue on this road for another 10 miles and arrive at the camp on both sides of the road.

COMMENTS: As you arrive at this campground there will be very large area on the left side of the road with at least 25 sites spread out all over the place. There are 2 sites with tables, rock fire rings, toilet and a boat launch. Some of the sites are on or close to the river. On the other side of the road, there are about 12 sites with toilet, rock fire rings but no tables. Most of these sites are set on the river in a grove of Ponderosa Pines and all are somewhat close to one another. This is a nice place to hang out for a while.
Note: This campground can also be reached from Goldendale by traveling west on State Route 142 for about 11 miles and bearing right onto the Goldendale-Glenwood Highway then 10 miles to the site entrance. **Discover Pass**

TURKEY HOLE   (VANCOUVER)

Number of sites: 12
Toilets: yes
Tables: no
Fishing: yes
Handicap Access: no

Type: tents; small trailers
Setting: river; forest
Fire: fire rings
Hiking: yes
Elevation: 385 feet

GPS: Lat: 45.7398577   Long: -121.2283982

DIRECTIONS: [KLICKITAT] From Vancouver Washington, follow Highway 14 East along the Columbia River to the small town of Lyle. This drive is about 75 miles. At Lyle, take a left onto State Route 142. Continue on this road for about 4.5 miles and take a left into the campground. There is no sign on the road so heads up. You can see the toilet from the road.

COMMENTS: This campsite offers a toilet and rock fire rings but no tables. There are some 12-15 sites for tents and small trailers some close to the Klickitat River and others further back. This site is not far off the road but appears to be pretty quiet. Nice little spot not far from the Columbia River. **Note:** This camp may also be reached from the town Goldendale by traveling west on SR 142 for 11 miles, and bearing left staying on State Highway 142 going south. **Discover Pass**

> *"Man masters nature not by force, but by understanding"*
>
> *~ Jacob Brownowski*

MINERAL SPRINGS CAMPSITE   **(VANCOUVER)**

Number of sites: 15   Type: tents; small trailers
Toilets: yes   Setting: river; forest
Tables: no   Fire: fire rings
Fishing: yes   Hiking: yes
Handicap Access: yes   Elevation: 550 feet
       GPS: Lat: 45.82036037   Long: -121.1176045

DIRECTIONS: [KLICKITAT] From Vancouver Washington, follow Highway 14 East along the Columbia River to the small town of Lyle. This drive is about 75 miles. At Lyle, take a left onto State Route 142. Continue on this road for about 15 miles and take a right at an unmarked gravel road. There is a large concrete block at the entrance road.

COMMENTS: This campsite features a handicap accessible toilet and rock fire rings but no tables. There are a good 15 spots to set up your tent or to pull in a small trailer. About half the sites set close to the river with the others setting back. The spots are good sized and set in a way to offer privacy. **Note:** These camps may also be reached from the town Goldendale by traveling west on SR 142 for 11 miles, and bearing left staying on State Highway 142 going south. **Discover Pass**

SPEARFISH CAMP   (VANCOUVER)

Number of sites: 2   Type: tents
Toilets: yes   Setting: river
Tables: yes   Fire: fire rings
Fishing: yes   Hiking: no
Handicap Access: no   Elevation: 400 feet
GPS: Lat: 45.61913   Long: -121.13975

DIRECTIONS: [KLICKITAT] From Vancouver, Follow Highway 14 East for about 75 miles to the small town of Lyle. From here continue on for about 9 miles and take a right at the road sign for The Dalles Lock & Dam. Follow this road about 2 miles and take a left at the sign for "Industrial Park" and Spearfish Lake. Continue on where in .5 miles road goes to gravel and in another .5 miles you'll see the camp entrance on the left.

COMMENTS: There are 2 camp spots here where you are required to carry your gear a very short distance. You'll find a vault toilet, tables, fire rings and a boat launch, but not much shade. There is also a picnic area with a table and fire ring that sets out away from the 2 campsites. This would make a good camp for fishermen and windsurfers. Set near Lake Celilo.

"Take care of the land, and it will take care of you. Take what you need from the land, but need what you take"

- Aboriginal law

AVERY PARK (VANCOUVER)

Number of sites: 6
Toilets: yes
Tables: yes
Fishing: yes
Handicap Access: no

Type: tents; small trailers
Setting: river
Fire: fire grates
Hiking: no
Elevation: 480 feet

GPS: Lat: 45.662182 Long: -121.036408

DIRECTIONS: [KLICKITAT] From Vancouver, Follow Highway 14 East for about 75 miles to the small town of Lyle. From here continue on for another 15 miles or so and take a right at the Avery Park sign. Follow this road down to the camp.

COMMENTS: Here you will find 6 campsites, 4 on the waterside and the other 2 across on the other side of the entrance road. All the sites are close together with tables, fire grates; vault toilet and boat launch area. This would be another good camp for fishermen and windsurfers. Not a lot of shade. **Note:** Avery Park is now an in lieu fishing site. It is open to the public on "non Indian fishing days." For information on availability of these sites call: 503-808-4322

"A tree never hits an automobile except in self-defense"

- Author Unknown

JOHN DAY LOCK AND DAM   (VANCOUVER)

Number of sites: open   Type: tents; small trailers
Toilets: yes   Setting: river
Tables: no   Fire: fire rings
Fishing: yes   Hiking: no
Handicap Access: no   Elevation: 570 feet
               GPS: Lat: 45.713852   Long: -120.709877

DIRECTIONS: [KLICKITAT] From Vancouver, Follow Highway 14 East for about 75 miles to the small town of Lyle. From here continue on for about 25 miles and take a right at the John Day Lock & Dam sign. Continue on this road for about 2.5 miles past the aluminum plant staying to the right and down to the camp on the left.

COMMENTS: This is wide open camp set on the Columbia River. There is a vault toilet but no tables and no trees. This camp is pretty much set up for self contained vehicles although to the north is an area with some small trees that might work for tents. If you fish or windsurf this could work for you.

ROCK CREEK BOAT LAUNCH   (VANCOUVER)

Number of sites: 5   Type: tents; small trailers
Toilets: yes   Setting: creek
Tables: no   Fire: fire rings
Fishing: yes   Hiking: no
Handicap Access: no   Elevation: 360 feet
                    GPS: Not Available

DIRECTIONS: [KLICKITAT] From Vancouver, Washington, Follow Highway 14 East for about 75 miles to the small town of Lyle. From here continue on for about 36 miles and take a left onto the Rock Creek Road. Continue on this road for about 1.5 miles and take a left into the site.

COMMENTS: This camp sets on Rock Creek which forms a small lake before it flows into the Columbia River. There is a large black top parking area at the boat launch with a toilet. You'll find about 4 or 5 tent sites set in an open area with some but not much shade. If you follow the camp entrance road staying to the right there is another lone site next to a now closed bathroom. This is a greener area with some shade. There are no tables at any of the sites.

SUNDALE PARK   (VANCOUVER)

Number of sites: 4   Type: tents; small trailers
Toilets: yes   Setting: river
Tables: yes   Fire: fire grates
Fishing: yes   Hiking: no
Handicap Access: yes   Elevation: 330 feet
              GPS: Lat: 45.7183 Long: -120.318359

DIRECTIONS: [KLICKITAT] From Vancouver, Washington. Follow Highway 14 East for about 75 miles to the small town of Lyle. From here continue on for about 39 miles and take a right into to Sundale Park.

COMMENTS: This camp offers 4 sites with picnic tables, accessible toilet, bar-b-que stands and a boat launch. There is a large parking area for folks with trailers. All 4 sites are close together with not much shade and pretty close to the train tracks. **Note:** Sundale Park is now an in lieu fishing site. It is open to the public on "non Indian fishing days." For information on availability of these sites call: 503-808-4322

ROOSEVELT PARK   (VANCOUVER)

Number of sites: 7   Type: tents
Toilets: yes   Setting: river
Tables: no   Fire: fire rings
Fishing: yes   Hiking: no
Handicap Access: no   Elevation: 340 feet
              GPS: Lat: 45.732449 Long: -120.22049

DIRECTIONS: [KLICKITAT] From Vancouver, Washington, Follow Highway 14 East for about 75 miles to the small town of Lyle. From here continue on for about 44 miles and take a right at Ferry Road. Follow this road for about a mile and take a left into the park. Continue on, passing the park campground on the left, which is fee, to the end of the road.

COMMENTS: There is room for about 7 tents on the right side of the road in the trees. A vault toilet can be found in the parking area above the tent area. No tables but there is a boat launch. You'll see a mini-mart on the Highway 14 when you make your turn onto Ferry Road. **Note:** There is camping at the park with tables, fire grates and toilets. I believe the fee is around ten dollars a night.

COUNCIL LAKE   (TROUT LAKE)

Number of sites: 7   Type: tents
Toilets: yes   Setting: forest; lake
Tables: no   Fire: fire grates
Fishing: yes   Hiking: yes
Handicap Access: no   Elevation: 4220 feet
           GPS: Lat: 46.266884   Long: -121.629982

DIRECTIONS: [LEWIS] From Trout Lake, travel north on the Mt. Adams Recreational Highway, for about 1.5 miles and at the junction with forest roads #23 and #80, bear left onto forest road #23. Continue on this road until you come to the junction with forest road #90. At this point you want to stay on road #23 which soon turns to gravel. Keep going until you reach forest road #2334 and take a left. Follow this road on into the site.

COMMENTS: This a beautiful green colored lake with the campsites set nearby. Some of the camps are small spaces and others are large. Either way, this is a very beautiful spot, quiet and peaceful.

SMOKEY CREEK   (TROUT LAKE)

Number of sites: 5   Type: tents, small trailers
Toilets: yes   Setting: forest; creek
Tables: yes   Fire: fire grates
Fishing: yes   Hiking: yes
Handicap Access: no   Elevation: 3670 feet
           GPS: Lat: 46.03132   Long: -121.688244

DIRECTIONS: [SKAMANIA] From Trout Lake, follow Highway 141 for 4.3 miles to a "Y" and bear right and stay on the pavement. In another 1.5 miles Highway 141 ends and Forest Service Road 24 begins. Continue on for another 2.5 miles to the junction with Forest Service Road 60 and take a right staying on Forest Service Road 24. Follow this road for 5.2 miles to the Smokey Creek forest camp on both sides of road.

COMMENTS: This campground is the first of many to be found in this area. It is wooded and is set next to a creek. There are trails nearby for hiking, bike riding, and horseback riding. Berry picking in season.

LITTLE GOOSE HORSECAMP   **(TROUT LAKE)**

Number of sites: 5   Type: tents, small trailers
Toilets: yes   Setting: forest; creek
Tables: yes   Fire: fire grates
Fishing: yes   Hiking: no
Handicap Access: no   Elevation: 4000 feet
        GPS: Lat: 46.03508   Long: -121.71377

DIRECTIONS: [SKAMANIA] From Trout Lake, follow Highway 141 for 4.3 miles to a "Y" and bear right and stay on the pavement. In another 1.5 miles Highway 141 ends and Forest Service Road 24 begins. Continue on for another 2.5 miles to the junction with Forest Service Road 60 and take a right staying on Forest Service Road 24. Follow this road for about 6.7 miles to campground on your left.

COMMENTS: 7 campsites located near the Little Goose Campground and near the northeastern boundary of Indian Heavens Wilderness. Several hiking or horse riding trails are in the area. Trailhead accessed in the campground.

LITTLE GOOSE   **(TROUT LAKE)**

Number of sites: 4   Type: tents, small trailers
Toilets: yes   Setting: forest; creek
Tables: yes   Fire: fire grates
Fishing: yes   Hiking: yes
Handicap Access: no   Elevation: 4000 feet
        GPS: Lat: 46.038007   Long: -121.712568

DIRECTIONS: [SKAMANIA] From Trout Lake, follow Highway 141 for 4.3 miles to a "Y' and bear right and stay on the pavement. In another 1.5 miles Highway 141 ends and Forest Service Road 24 begins. Continue on for another 2.5 miles to the junction with Forest Service Road 60 and take a right staying on Forest Service Road 24. Follow this road for about 6.8 miles to the campground.

COMMENTS: 4 primitive rustic campsites located near Indian Heaven Wilderness. A horse camp is located across the road and has hiking and horse riding trail access to the wilderness. Berry picking in season. Other trailheads are nearby.

86

MEADOW CREEK INDIAN CAMP   (TROUT LAKE)

Number of sites: 4
Toilets: yes
Tables: yes
Fishing: yes
Handicap Access: no

Type: tents, small trailers
Setting: forest
Fire: fire grates
Hiking: yes
Elevation: 4100 feet

GPS: Lat: 46.135704   Long: -121.493895

DIRECTIONS: [SKAMANIA] From Trout Lake, follow Highway 141 for 4.3 miles to a "Y" and bear right and stay on the pavement. In another 1.5 miles Highway 141 ends and Forest Service Road 24 begins. Continue on for another 2.5 miles to the junction with Forest Service Road 60 and take a right, staying on Forest Service Road 24. Follow this road for about 10.8 miles to the campground.

COMMENTS: Traditional Native American Indian camp located close to the Sawtooth Mountain berry fields. Dispersed camping area with 3 sites popular during berry picking season. Public can pick berries only on the west side of Forest Service Road 24. Access to a Indian Heaven Wilderness hiking trail is several miles north.

87

COLD SPRINGS INDIAN CAMP   (TROUT LAKE)

Number of sites: 5   Type: tents, small trailers
Toilets: yes   Setting: forest; mountain
Tables: yes   Fire: fire grates
Fishing: no   Hiking: yes
Handicap Access: no   Elevation: 3900 feet
              GPS: Lat: 46.080584   Long: -121.752108

DIRECTIONS: [SKAMANIA] From Trout Lake, follow Highway 141 for 4.3 miles to a "Y" and bear right and stay on the pavement. In another 1.5 miles Highway 141 ends and Forest Service Road 24 begins. Continue on for another 2.5 miles to the junction with Forest Service Road 60 and take a right staying on Forest Service Road 24. Follow this road for about 11.4 miles to the campground entrance on your right. Then follow this road .5 miles to the site.

COMMENTS: Traditional Native American Indian camp located close to the Sawtooth Mountain berry fields. Dispersed camping area with 5 sites popular during berry picking season. Public can pick berries only on the west side of Forest Service Road 24. Access to a Indian Heaven Wilderness hiking trail is several miles north This campground is really off the beaten path. The views are great, the campsites large and private.

"Keep a green tree in your heart and perhaps a singing bird will come"

~ Chinese proverb

SURPRISE LAKES   (TROUT LAKE)

Number of sites: 25   Type: tents, small trailers
Toilets: yes   Setting: forest; lake
Tables: yes   Fire: fire grates
Fishing: yes   Hiking: yes
Handicap Access: no   Elevation: 4260 feet
GPS: Lat: 46.091400   Long: -121.759442

DIRECTIONS: [SKAMANIA] From Trout Lake, follow Highway 141 for 4.3 miles to a "Y", and bear right and stay on the pavement. In another 1.5 miles Highway 141 ends and Forest Service Road 24 begins. Keep going for 2.5 miles to the junction with Forest Service Road 60 and take a right staying on Forest Service Road 24. Follow this road for about 12.1 miles and take a right at unsigned gravel road.

COMMENTS: Can't say for sure how many campsites there are here, only that there are many. Some are on the lake and others away from the lake. Some have tables, some don't. What I can say is that this is one beautiful area. Hiking, swimming, fishing, and boating should keep you busy here. **Note:** Another .5 miles up Road 24, you'll come to the Middle Creek Trail 26. If you take a right here, you'll find a small lake with 1 campsite, fire ring and a table all set on a little meadow.

> *"Even the sick should try these so-called dangerous passes, because for every unfortunate they kill, they cure a thousand"*
>
> *~John Muir*

Number of sites: 8	Type: tents
Toilets: yes	Setting: forest; mountain
Tables: yes	Fire: fire grates
Fishing: no	Hiking: yes
Handicap Access: no	Elevation: 4030 feet

GPS: Lat: 46.112234 Long: -121.766977

DIRECTIONS: [SKAMANIA] From Trout Lake, follow Highway 141 for 4.3 miles to a "Y", bear right and stay on the pavement. In another 1.5 miles, Highway 141 ends and Forest Service Road 24 begins. Keep going for 2.5 miles to the junction with Forest Service Road 60 and take a right staying on Forest Service Road 24. Follow this road for about 13 miles or so where you will come to a junction with Forest Service Road 30. Take a right on Road 24 and then in just a bit, take another right onto Forest Service Road 2480 and follow this for .3 miles to the campground on your right.

COMMENTS: 8 small forested campsites better suited to tent camping. Located north of Indian Heaven Wilderness and west of the Pacific Crest Trail. Activities include hiking, and berry picking in season.

SADDLE

Number of sites: 8
Toilets: yes
Tables: yes
Fishing: no
Handicap Access: no

Type: tents
Setting: forest; mountain
Fire: fire grates
Hiking: yes
Elevation: 4240 feet

GPS: Lat: 46.118245   Long: -121.76242

DIRECTIONS: [SKAMANIA] From Trout Lake, follow Highway 141 for 4.3 miles to a "Y", bear right and stay on the pavement. In another 1.5 miles, Highway 141 ends and Forest Service Road 24 begins. Keep going for 2.5 miles to a junction with Forest Service Road 60 and take a right staying on Road 24. Follow this road for about 13 miles or so where you come to a junction with Forest Service Road 30. Take a right staying on Forest Service Road 24 and then in just a little bit take another right onto Road 2480 and continue on for .8 miles to the campground.

COMMENTS: This is another high altitude campground that is set in deep forest. Best for tent camping, there are trails in the area and berry picking in season very peaceful, with lots of trees.

Number of sites: 5   Type: tents
Toilets: yes   Setting: forest
Tables: yes   Fire: fire grates
Fishing: no   Hiking: yes
Handicap Access: no   Elevation: 3800 feet
       GPS: Lat: 46.123492   Long: -121.779098

DIRECTIONS: [SKAMANIA] From Trout Lake, follow Highway 141 for 4.3 miles to a "Y", bear right and stay on the pavement. In another 1.5 miles, Highway 141 ends and Forest Service Road 24 begins. Keep going for 2.5 miles to the junction with Forest Service Road 60 and take a right staying on Road 24. Follow this road for 13 miles or so to the junction with Forest Service Road 30. Take a right staying on Forest Service Road 24 and go about 1.5 miles to the campground entrance on your left.

COMMENTS: 15 lightly used campsites located near berry fields. You'll find a hiking trail leading out from the campground with access to other forest trails. Mountain biking, hiking, and horse riding on the trail. Activities include berry picking in season. **NWFP**

"You can't study the darkness by flooding it with light"

~Edward Abbey

STEAMBOAT LAKE   (TROUT LAKE)

Number of sites: 20   Type: tents
Toilets: yes   Setting: forest; lake
Tables: yes   Fire: rock fire rings
Fishing: yes   Hiking: yes
Handicap Access: no   Elevation: 3700 feet
        GPS: Lat: 46.132339   Long: -121.715361

DIRECTIONS: [SKAMANIA] From Trout Lake, follow Highway 141 for about 1.7 miles and turn left onto Forest Service Road 88. Continue on this road for about 21 miles and take a left onto a road signed "Steamboat Lake". Follow this, sometimes on a rough road, 3 miles to the site.

COMMENTS: Upon entering the campground, you want to take a left and go past the sites above the lake and follow this dirt road around to the many campsites around the lake, some with tables. This lake offers fishing and canoeing, with hiking an added bonus. This is a very beautiful spot.

BERRY FIELD ACCESS   (TROUT LAKE)

Number of sites: 20   Type: tents, small trailers
Toilets: yes   Setting: forest
Tables: yes   Fire: fire grates
Fishing: no   Hiking: yes
Handicap Access: yes   Elevation: 3800 feet
        GPS: Lat: 46.087172   Long: -121.794225

DIRECTIONS: [SKAMANIA] From Trout Lake, follow Highway 141 for about 1.7 miles and turn left onto Forest Service Road 88. Continue on this road for about 7.8 miles and take another left onto Forest Service Road 8851. Follow this road for 3.4 miles and bear left onto Forest Service Road 24. Continue on for another 4 miles and take a right onto Forest Service Road 30. Keep going on this road for 1.4 miles then take a left onto Forest Service Road 580. From here it is about 1.4 miles to the site.

COMMENTS: This is an unusual spot. There is a large paved parking area for trailers and also areas in the trees for tents. There are trails at the site leading into the berry fields. September is berry-picking time. The Pacific Crest Trail also passes through here

WICKY SHELTER   (TROUT LAKE)

Number of sites: 6   Type: tents, small trailers
Toilets: yes   Setting: forest; creek
Tables: yes   Fire: fire grates
Fishing: yes   Hiking: yes
Handicap Access: no   Elevation: 3600 feet
        GPS: Lat: 46.092135   Long: -121.532575

DIRECTIONS: [SKAMANIA] From Trout Lake, travel north on the Mt. Adams Recreational Highway for about 1.4 miles to a "Y" and bear right. In another .5 miles, you come to another Y. This time, bear left, onto Forest Service Road 80. Continue on for 3.7 miles where there is another "Y" and bear right onto Forest Service Road 8040, which is gravel. Keep going for 1.8 miles to the campground on your left.

COMMENTS: A small primitive dispersed tent camping site with a small shelter just off of the road. RV's can park in front of the shelter. Mount Adams Wilderness is to the north for hiking and horse riding.

MORRISON CREEK (TROUT LAKE)

Number of sites: 8
Toilets: yes
Tables: yes
Fishing: yes
Handicap Access: yes

Type: tents, small trailers
Setting: forest; creek
Fire: fire grates
Hiking: yes
Elevation: 4600 feet

GPS: Lat: 46.135704 Long: -121.493895

DIRECTIONS: [SKAMANIA] From Trout Lake, travel north on the Mt. Adams Recreational Highway, for about 1.4 miles to a "Y" and bear right. In another .5 miles, you come to another Y. This time, bear left, onto Forest Service Road 80. Continue on for 3.7 miles where there is another "Y" and bear right onto Forest Service Road 8040, which is gravel. Continue on for 3.7 miles to the campground.

COMMENTS: This site was burned over in the Cascade Creek fire of 2012. Several primitive camp sites are available, some along Morrison Creek. The site serves as a trailhead to the Shorthorn Trail #16 which enters Mount Adams Wilderness, **NWFP**

COLD SPRINGS (TROUT LAKE)

Number of sites: 12
Toilets: yes
Tables: yes
Fishing: no
Handicap Access: no

Type: tents
Setting: forest; mountain
Fire: fire grates
Hiking: yes
Elevation: 5500 feet

GPS: Lat: 46.1365 Long. -121.4965

DIRECTIONS: [SKAMANIA] From Trout Lake, take the Mount Adams Recreational Highway north for about 1.4 miles and bear right at the "Y". In .5 miles or so you'll come to another "Y" and this time bear left onto Forest Service Road 80. Follow this road for 3.7 miles and bear right onto Forest Service Road 8040. Continue on this road for 3.7 miles to the Morrison Creek campground and take a right. Follow this road another 2.8 miles to the campground.

COMMENTS: This rather large campground is used primarily for backpacking trips into the Mount Adams Wilderness and climbing Mount Adams. The road in is fairly rough and not recommended for trailers. The campground is set at 5500 feet. **NWFP**

TWIN FALLS   (TROUT LAKE)

Number of sites: 5   Type: tents
Toilets: yes   Setting: forest; creek; waterfalls
Tables: yes   Fire: fire grates
Fishing: yes   Hiking: no
Handicap Access: no   Elevation: 2700 feet
        GPS: Lat: 46.215808   Long: -121.668277

DIRECTIONS: [SKAMANIA] From Trout Lake, travel north on the Mount Adams Recreational Highway for about 1.4 miles to the junction with Forest Service Road 23 and bear left onto Road 23. Follow this road for about 20 miles to the junction with Forest Service Road 90 and go left again onto Road 90. Continue on this road for about 7 miles and take a left on Forest Service Road 560 into the campground. **Note:** There isn't a sign at the campground entrance and the Forest Service Road 560 sign is hard to see, so you want to take your left into the campground just before reaching the milepost sign 42.

COMMENTS: A small, less developed campground for tent camping only, located at the confluence of Twin Falls Creek and the Lewis River. The campground is placed on the banks of the river with an impressive view of the falls. Twin Falls campground is a little hard to find but well worth the effort. The falls aren't real high but very powerful. Here you need to park in the parking area and carry your gear a short distance. Sleep to the roar of the falls. Nearby is the Summit Prairie Trail #2.

LEWIS RIVER HORSECAMP   (TROUT LAKE)

Number of sites: 5   Type: tents, small trailers
Toilets: yes   Setting: forest
Tables: yes   Fire: fire grates
Fishing: yes   Hiking: yes
Handicap Access: yes   Elevation: 1900 feet
              GPS: Lat: 46.185325   Long: -121.851075

DIRECTIONS: [SKAMANIA] From Trout Lake, travel north on Mt. Adams Recreational Highway for about 1.4 miles to the junction with Forest Service Road 23 and bear left onto Road 23. Follow this road for about 20 miles to the junction with Forest Service Road 90 and go left again onto Road 90. Continue on this road for about 16.5 miles to Forest Service Road 9300 and take a right. Continue on .3 miles to campground.

COMMENTS: This campground has a large parking area for trailer camping, and has horse corrals. Some sites are in the trees for shade, others in the sun. Hiking and horseback riding are options. **Note:** about .3 miles before arriving at Road 9300 and just before the bridge over Quartz Creek, there are a couple of campsites on the right side of the road. These sites have one table but no toilets and they are right on Quartz Creek. **NWFP**

OUTLOOK CREEK   (GLENWOOD)

Number of sites: 10   Type: tents
Toilets: yes   Setting: forest; creek
Tables: 3   Fire: fire rings
Fishing: yes   Hiking: yes
Handicap Access: no   Elevation: 1800 feet
              GPS: Lat: 46.015816   Long: -121.219841

DIRECTIONS: [KLICKITAT] From Glenwood, travel about 2.5 miles east on Highway 142 and on the right you'll see the campground entrance. There is no sign to speak of and the site is un-named.

COMMENTS: There are about 10 sites scattered throughout the forest, 3 with tables. There are also two toilets. A pretty little stream runs nearby a couple of the sites.

BIRD CREEK   (GLENWOOD)

Number of sites: 8   Type: tents, small trailers
Toilets: yes   Setting: forest; creek
Tables: yes   Fire: fire grates
Fishing: yes   Hiking: yes
Handicap Access: no   Elevation: 2400 feet
          GPS: Lat: 46.0637331   Long: -121.3375783

DIRECTIONS: [KLICKITAT] From Glenwood, head west through town and in about .3 miles turn right onto the Bird Creek Road. Follow this road for less than a mile and take a left over the cattle guard then a quick right onto the Bird Creek-K-3000 Road. Continue on for 1.3 miles to another junction and take a right. Follow this road for a couple of miles to the K-4000 Road and take a left. Go for about 2 miles on this road to the campground entrance on your left then continue on for about .2 miles to the site.

COMMENTS: This is a large open campground set on Bird Creek. Located on the east side of Mount Adams, Bird Creek Campground offers visitors a relaxing and natural setting to come home to after exploring the area's unique volcanic geology. **Discover Pass**

ISLAND CAMP CAMPGROUND   (GLENWOOD)

Number of sites: 6
Toilets: yes
Tables: yes
Fishing: yes
Handicap Access: yes

Type: tents; small trailers
Setting: forest; creek
Fire: fire grates
Hiking: yes
Elevation: 2550 feet

GPS: Lat: 46.04907   Long: -121.22805

DIRECTIONS: [KLICKITAT] From Glenwood, head west through town and in about .3 miles turn right onto the Bird Creek Road. Follow this road for less than a mile and take a left over the cattle guard then a quick right onto the Bird Creek-K-3000 Road. Continue on for 1.3 miles to another junction and take a right. Follow this road for a couple of miles to the K-4000 Road and take a left. Go for about 2 miles on this road to the Bird Creek Campground and take a left into campground and over the bridge and in about 1 mile take a right and travel 2.5 miles to the Island Camp Campground.

COMMENTS: Island camp, along Bird Creek, is a perfect home base for exploring Mount Adams. Island Camp is in a forested area and provides many recreation opportunities for visitors to take advantage of including checking out the lava tubes and blow holes nearby. Nice camp.
Discover Pass

> *"Look deep into nature, and then you will understand everything better"*
>
> *~Albert Einstein*

KEN WILCOX HORSECAMP   (WENATCHEE)

Number of sites: 20   Type: tents, small trailers
Toilets: yes   Setting: forest; meadow
Tables: yes   Fire: fire grates
Fishing: no   Hiking: yes
Handicap Access: no   Elevation: 5500 feet
                 GPS: Lat: 47.3135   Long: -120.535

DIRECTIONS: [KITTITAS] From Wenatchee, travel west on Highway's 97 and 2, for 15 miles to the junction with Highway 97 heading south toward Ellensburg. Follow this highway for about 23 miles and take a left onto Forest Service Road 9716 to Haney Meadows. Continue on this road for about 3.7 miles and take a left at the road signed Haney Meadows and Lion Rock. This is Forest Service Road 9712. In another 1.6 miles bear left at the "Y" and continue on another 3.3 miles to the campground.

COMMENTS: This campground is set in a beautiful forest and just across the road from Haney Meadow. The meadow is huge but do not ride or venture into Haney Meadows itself. What appears to be a tranquil meadow was once the scene of mining operations that left sink holes as a legacy. There is also an old log cabin on site that was built in 1933 complete with a story about the folks that built it. This campground is maintained by the Forest Service and the Washington Backcountry Horseman. **Note:** The last 3.3 miles can be rough, but it's worth the drive for the scenery. **NWFP**

LION ROCK

Number of sites: 3	Type: tents, small trailers
Toilets: yes	Setting: forest; mountain
Tables: yes	Fire: fire grates
Fishing: no	Hiking: yes
Handicap Access: no	Elevation: 6300 feet

GPS: Lat: 47.2512 Long: -120.5837

DIRECTIONS: [KITTITAS] From Wenatchee, travel west on Highway's 97 and 2, for 15 miles to the junction with Highway 97 heading south toward Ellensburg. Follow this highway for about 23 miles and take left onto Forest Service Road 9716 to Haney Meadows. Continue on this road for about 3.7 miles and take a left at the road signed Haney Meadows and Lion Rock. This is Forest Service Road 9712. In another 1.6 miles bear right at the "Y" and follow this road for about five miles to the campground entrance on the right.

COMMENTS: Another high mountain camp, this one offers great hiking and wonderful views. Just before entering the actual campground, there are some nice view camping areas to your left, some in the trees and some in the open. The road in to this site offers up wonderful views of Mount Rainier. **Note:** Continuing on Forest Service Road 9712 for another 30 miles or so will bring you to Highway 90 at Ellensburg.

"The butterfly counts not months but moments, and has time enough"

~ Rabindranath Tagore

TEANAWAY

Number of sites: 25
Toilets: yes
Tables: yes
Fishing: yes
Handicap Access: yes

Type: tents, small trailers
Setting: forest; river
Fire: rock fire rings
Hiking: yes
Elevation: 3500 feet

GPS: Lat: 47.2570644 Long: -120.8920268

DIRECTIONS: [KITTITAS] From Ellensburg, travel north on Highway 97 towards Wenatchee for 1 mile to a stop sign and take a left. Still on Highway 97, go another 1 mile to the junction with Highways 97 and 10 and stay straight following Highway 10. Follow this road for about 15 miles to the junction with Highway 970 west and east. Take a right heading east towards Wenatchee and continue on for 4.3 miles to the Teanaway River Road and take a left. Follow this road for 7.3 miles to the West Fork Teanaway River Road and take a left. Stay straight to the campground entrance on your left.

COMMENTS: Located along the west fork of the Teanaway River, this is a wide open campground with a lot of shade. Most of the sites on the river have tables.

Number of sites: 9	Type: tents, small trailers
Toilets: yes	Setting: forest; river
Tables: yes	Fire: fire grates
Fishing: yes	Hiking: yes
Handicap Access: yes	Elevation: 2000 feet

GPS: Lat: 47.2901189 Long: -120.9573069

DIRECTIONS: [KITTITAS] From Ellensburg, travel north on Highway 97 towards Wenatchee for 1 mile to stop sign and take a left. Still on Highway 97, go another 1 mile to the junction with Highways 97 and 10 and stay straight following Highway 10. Continue on this road for about 15 miles to the junction with Highway 970 east and west. Take a right heading east towards Wenatchee and continue on for 4.3 miles to Teanaway River Road and take a left. Follow this road for 7.3 miles and turn left onto the West Fork Teanaway River Road. Take your first right and in 2.6 miles the pavement ends. Another 1 mile and you arrive at the campground on your left.

COMMENTS: Located along the middle fork of the Teanaway River, the camp offers 9 campsites with fire rings and two group campsites with fire rings, and a toilet. This is a nice place to spend some time.

> *"Man did not weave the web of life...he is merely a strand in that web...whatever he does to the web...he does to himself"*
> ~ *Chief Seattle*

29 PINES

Number of sites: 45
Toilets: yes
Tables: yes
Fishing: yes
Handicap Access: no

Type: tents, small trailers
Setting: forest; river
Fire: fire grates
Hiking: yes
Elevation: 2620 feet

GPS: Lat: 47.328811   Long: -120.854172

DIRECTIONS: [KITTITAS] From Ellensburg, travel north on Highway 97 towards Wenatchee for 1 mile to a stop sign and take a left. Still on highway 97, go another 1 mile to the junction with Highways 97 and 10 and stay straight following Highway 10. Continue on this road for about 15 miles to the junction with Highway 970 west and east. Take a right heading east towards Wenatchee and continue on for 4.3 miles to the Teanaway River Road and take a left. Follow this road for 13 miles to the campground on your left.

COMMENTS: This is a very large campground with many sites on the Teanaway River. This is a good camp for folks with children. There's easy access, right off the paved road.

DE ROUX

Number of sites: 5
Toilets: yes
Tables: yes
Fishing: yes
Handicap Access: no

Type: tents
Setting: forest; river
Fire: fire grates
Hiking: yes
Elevation: 3760 feet

GPS: Lat: 47.417492 Long: -120.937019

DIRECTIONS: [KITTITAS] From Ellensburg, travel north on Highway 97 towards Wenatchee for one mile to a stop sign and take a left. Still on Highway 97, go another 1 mile to the junction with Highway 97 and 10 and stay straight following Highway 10. Continue on this road for about 15 miles to the junction with Highway 970 west and east. Take a right heading east towards Wenatchee and continue on for about 4.3 miles and turn left on the Teanaway River Road. Follow this road for just over 13 miles and then bear right onto the Forest Service Road 9737. Keep going on this road for 1.4 miles then bear left at the "Y". Continue on for another 5 miles to the campground on your left. **Note:** after passing Wahoo camp, De Roux is your next left.

COMMENTS: De Roux is a small Campground and trailhead situated on De Roux Creek and North Fork Teanaway River. There is a hiking and horse riding trail which connects to another trail leading into the Alpine Wilderness. Used mostly by horse riders, the camp includes hitching rails and camping areas big enough for horses. Fishing in the river and creeks.

FISH LAKE   (CLE ELUM)

Number of sites: 4   Type: tents
Toilets: yes   Setting: forest; lake
Tables: yes   Fire: fire grates
Fishing: yes   Hiking: yes
Handicap Access: no   Elevation: 3400 feet
GPS: Lat: 47.5239   Long: -121.073

DIRECTIONS: [KITTITAS] From Cle Elum, Follow Highway 903 towards the town of Roslyn. Continue on through the town of Roslyn, staying on Highway 903. In about 8.7 miles, Highway 903 ends. Keep going, and in 11.5 miles, you want to bear right at the "Y" up the gravel road. This is Forest Service Road 4330. Continue on and in another 2.5 miles, stay left and follow this road another 7 miles to Scatter Creek. Cross the creek and travel another mile to the campground on your right.

COMMENTS: This campground is located right at the Fish Lake guard station. It sits in a wooded area overlooking Fish Lake.   Just after crossing Scatter Creek, there is a camping area on your left with fire rings.   A little further on, towards Fish Lake, there are some other campsites at Tucqula Lake on your left. You'll find a vault toilet between these two primitive camping areas to the right. These are very remote and beautiful spots. Bring your canoe.

RED TOP CAMPGROUND   (CLE ELUM)

Number of sites: 3   Type: tents
Toilets: yes   Setting: forest; mountain
Tables: yes   Fire: fire grates
Fishing: no   Hiking: yes
Handicap Access: no   Elevation: 5100 feet
GPS: Lat: 47.2982   Long: -120.761

DIRECTIONS: [KITTITAS] From Cle Elum, travel Highway 97 for about 28 miles and take a left onto Forest Service Road 9738. Follow this road and then take Forest Service Road 9720 to its end.

COMMENTS: 3 dispersed campsites without facilities are on Red Top Mountain. Hiking only trailhead and viewpoint. There is rock hounding in the neighborhood. **NWFP**

RIDERS CAMP

Number of sites: 12
Toilets: yes
Tables: yes
Fishing: no
Handicap Access: no

Type: tents, small trailers
Setting: forest
Fire: rock fire rings
Hiking: yes
Elevation: 4400 feet

GPS: Lat: 47.0291 Long: -120.936

DIRECTIONS: [KITTITAS] FROM Highway 90 at Ellensburg, take exit 106. Coming from the west, take a right at the bottom of the off ramp. Coming from the east, go left and continue on over the bridge. You'll see a K.O.A. campground on your left. This puts you on the Thorp Highway. Follow this road for 3.3 miles to Cove Road and take a left. In another 1 mile you'll come to an intersection and you want to stay straight on Cove Road. Follow this road for another 3 miles to the Manastash Road and take a right. In another 7.5 miles, the pavement ends, and you are now on Forest Service Road 31. Continue on for 9.6 miles to Riders camp.

COMMENTS: Dispersed camping for campers, groups, or campers with horses is located close to a creek with stock water available from the seasonal creek. Large enough for 20-50 people per group. Camping with OHV's permitted. Hiking, horse riding, mountain biking, and OHV trails are in this area. Some picnic tables provided. **NWFP**

"Rivers and rocks and trees have always been talking to us, but we've forgotten how to listen"

~Michael Roads

MANASTASH

Number of sites: 40
Toilets: yes
Tables: no
Fishing: no
Handicap Access: yes

Type: tents, small trailers
Setting: forest
Fire: rock fire rings
Hiking: yes
Elevation: 4400 feet

GPS: Lat: 47.0345 Long: -120.954

DIRECTIONS: [KITTITAS] From Highway 90 at Ellensburg, take exit 106. Coming from the west take a right at the bottom of the off ramp. Coming from the east, take a left and continue on over the bridge, which puts you on the Thorp Highway. Follow this road for 3.3 miles to the Cove Road and take a left. In another 1 mile you'll come to an intersection where you want to go straight on the Cove Road. Continue on for another 3 miles and take a right onto the Manastash Road. Follow this road, and in 7.5 miles the pavement ends and you are now on Forest Service Road 31. Keep going, and in about 10 miles you'll come to a "Y" and you want to bear left onto Forest Service Road 3104 then take a right to the site.

COMMENTS: Many campsites and an improved dispersed camping area for groups over 50 people. OHV's allowed. Group site accommodates RV's, trailers, and tents. Hiking, horse riding, and mountain biking trails are nearby. OHV trails are in the vicinity. **NWFP**

QUARTZ MOUNTAIN   (ELLENSBURG)

Number of sites: 2   Type: tents
Toilets: yes   Setting: forest
Tables: yes   Fire: fire grates
Fishing: no   Hiking: yes
Handicap Access: no   Elevation: 6200 feet
GPS: Lat: 47.0767   Long: -121.08

DIRECTIONS: [KITTITAS] From Highway 90 at Ellensburg, take exit 106. If coming from the west, take a right at the bottom of the off ramp. Coming from the east, go left and continue on over the bridge. You are now on Thorp Highway. Continue on this road for 3.3 miles to the Cove Road and take a left. In another 1 mile you'll come to an intersection and you want to stay straight on the Cove Road. Keep going and in 3 miles take a right onto the Manastash Road. Follow this road for 7.5 miles, where the pavement ends. You are now on Forest Service Road 31. Continue on this road for about 10.5 miles to a "T", and take a left. Stay straight and in another 3.8 miles bear left at the "Y". One mile further brings you to another "Y" and bear left again. Follow this road for 3.5 miles to the campground.

COMMENTS: This is small campground set above 6000 feet near a meadow and great views. You're likely to have not much company here. **NWFP**

109

TAMARACK SPRINGS (ELLENSBURG)

Number of sites: 3
Toilets: yes
Tables: yes
Fishing: no
Handicap Access: no

Type: tents
Setting: forest
Fire: fire grates
Hiking: yes
Elevation: 4700 feet

GPS: Lat: 47.063896 Long: -120.897846

DIRECTIONS: [KITTITAS] From Highway 90 at Ellensburg, take exit 106. If coming from the west, take a right at the bottom of the off ramp. From the east, go left and continue on over the bridge. You are now on the Thorp Highway. Follow this road for 3.3 miles and take a left onto the Cove Road. In another 1 mile, you come to an intersection where you want to stay straight on the Cove Road. Continue on for 3 miles and take a right onto the Manastash Road. In 7.5 miles the pavement ends and you are now on Forest Service Road 31. Keep going on this road for about 10.5 miles to the junction with Forest Service Road 3120 and take a right. Follow this road for another 4 miles to the junction with Forest Service Road 3330 and stay to the right on Road 3120. In another couple of miles you arrive at the entrance to Tamarack Springs. Follow this road to the site

COMMENTS: This campground, another lightly used spot is set in the woods with a trailhead for hikers and horseback riding. There is also a corral for horses. **NWFP**

> *"Some national parks have long waiting lists for camping reservations. When you have to wait a year to sleep next to a tree, something is wrong"*
>
> *~George Carlin*

SOUTH FORK MEADOWS (ELLENSBURG)

Number of sites: 3
Toilets: yes
Tables: yes
Fishing: no
Handicap Access: no

Type: tents
Setting: meadow
Fire: fire grates
Hiking: yes
Elevation: 2800 feet

GPS: Lat: 47.095139   Long: -120.987022

DIRECTIONS: [KITTITAS] From Highway 90 at Ellensburg, take exit 106. If coming from the west, take a right at the bottom of the off ramp. From the east go left and continue on over the bridge. You are now on the Thorp Highway. Follow this road for 3.3 miles and take a left onto the Cove Road. In another 1 mile, come to an intersection and stay straight. Continue on for 3 miles and take a right at the Manastash Road. In 7.5 miles the pavement ends and you are now on Forest Service Road 31. Keep going on this road for about 10.5 miles to the junction with Forest Service Road 3120 and take a right. Follow this road for about 4 miles to the junction with Forest Service Road 3330 and bear left onto Road 3330. Stay on this road for about 8.5 miles where you come to a "T" and take a left. In another 1.3 miles, take another left on a road signed South Fork Meadow Campground. Follow this road for 4 miles to the campground entrance on your left, Forest Service Road 4322. Continue on .3 miles to campground.

COMMENTS: This site is set in a large meadow with lots of flowers and access to the South Fork Taneum Trail 1367. Stock water is available at the creek

.

AHTANUM MEADOWS (YAKIMA)

Number of sites: 5
Toilets: yes
Tables: yes
Fishing: yes
Handicap Access: yes

Type: tents; small trailers
Setting: forest; meadow; creek
Fire: fire grates
Hiking: yes
Elevation: 3070 feet

GPS: Lat: 46.5226204 Long: -121.0092422

DIRECTIONS: [YAKIMA] From Yakima, travel south on Highway 82 for about 3 miles to the Union Gap exit. At the bottom of the off ramp, take a right, and at the first stop light take a left. Continue on and at the next stop light, take a right. Follow this road for approximately 19 miles to the small town of Tampico, and bear right. Keep going, and in another 9 miles you'll arrive at the campground on your left.

COMMENTS: Set in a forested area with a stream running through the campground, Ahtanum Camp and is one of the most readily accessed camping areas in the Ahtanum State Forest. Located on the North Fork of Ahtanum Creek near the paved county road. **Discover Pass**

ANTANUM CAMP AND PICNIC AREA (YAKIMA)

Number of sites: 7
Toilets: yes
Tables: yes
Fishing: yes
Handicap Access: yes

Type: tents, small trailers
Setting: forest; creek
Fire: fire grates
Hiking: yes
Elevation: 3070 feet

GPS: Lat: Not Available

DIRECTIONS: [YAKIMA] From Yakima, travel south on Highway 82 for about 3 miles to the Union Gap exit. At the bottom of the off ramp, take a right, and at the first stop light take a left. Continue on and at the next stop light, take a right. Follow this road for approximately 19 miles to the small town of Tampico, and bear right. Keep going, and in another 9.5 miles you'll arrive at the campground on your left.

COMMENTS: Like Antanum Meadows campground, this one is also set in the forest with a stream. There are nice campsites, with hiking and fishing. **Discover Pass**

TREE PHONES

Number of sites: 14
Toilets: yes
Tables: yes
Fishing: yes
Handicap Access: yes

Type: tents, small trailers
Setting: forest; creek
Fire: fire grates
Hiking: yes
Elevation: 4835 feet

GPS: Lat: 46.4970635   Long: -121.1211881

DIRECTIONS: [YAKIMA] From Yakima, travel south on Highway 82 for about 3 miles to the Union Gap exit. At the bottom of the off ramp, take a right, and then a left at the first stop light. Continue on and at the next stop light take a right. Follow this road for approximately 19 miles to the small town of Tampico and bear right. Keep going, and in about 9.6 miles the pavement ends. From here, in .2 miles you'll come to a "Y" and bear right. Continue on for 5.7 miles to the campground on your left.

COMMENTS: This is Southwest Washington camping. Tree Phones Campground is highly popular among visitors. Near Darland Mountain, the camp provides access to the 23-mile Grey Rock Trail. This camp is set on a creek in a beautiful area. **Discover Pass**

CLOVER FLATS (YAKIMA)

Number of sites: 8
Toilets: yes
Tables: yes
Fishing: no
Handicap Access: yes

Type: tents, small trailers
Setting: forest; meadow,
Fire: fire grates
Hiking: yes
Elevation: 6345 feet

GPS: Lat: 46.30340   Long: -121.10688

DIRECTIONS: [YAKIMA] From Yakima, travel south on Highway 82 for about 3 miles to the Union Gap exit. At the bottom of the off ramp, take a right and then a left at the first stop light. Continue on and at the next stop light take a right. Follow this road approximately 19 miles to the small town of Tampico and bear right. Keep going, and in about 9.5 miles the pavement ends. From here, in .2 miles you'll come to a "Y" and you want to bear right. Continue on for another 8.5 miles or so to the camp entrance road on the left.

COMMENTS: This site is way up high in the mountains and is the westernmost camping facility on the Middle Fork Road. The campground is surrounded by meadow, wildflowers and mountains. It doesn't get much better than this. There are nearby hiking trails. **Discover Pass**

"What is the purpose of the giant sequoia tree?
The purpose of the giant sequoia tree is to provide shade for the tiny titmouse"

~Edward Abbey

Number of sites: 2   Type: tents
Toilets: yes   Setting: forest
Tables: yes   Fire: fire grates
Fishing: no   Hiking: yes
Handicap Access: no   Elevation: 6300 feet

GPS: Lat: Not Available

DIRECTIONS: [YAKIMA] From Yakima, travel south on Highway 82 for about 3 miles to the Union Gap exit. At the bottom of the off ramp take a right and then a left at the first stop light. Continue on, and at the next stop light, and take a right. Follow this road for approximately 19 miles to the small town of Tampico and bear right. Keep going, and just a little past the Ahtanum Meadows campground you want to bear right onto the North Fork Road. Follow this road and in 2 miles bear right at the "Y". Continue on for 2.3 miles to another "Y" and this time bear left. Continue on and in 1.3 miles you come to Grey Rock trailhead on your left.

COMMENTS: This is a small spot right off the side of the road, with room for a couple of tents. The Grey Rock Trail is a multi-use trail that meanders through a variety of forest types, including ponderosa pine forests, dense Douglas-fir stands and subalpine fir and spruce forests. **Discover Pass**

SNOW CABIN   (YAKIMA)

Number of sites: 8   Type: tents, small trailers
Toilets: yes   Setting: forest; meadow
Tables: yes   Fire: fire grates
Fishing: no   Hiking: yes
Handicap Access: no   Elevation: 6500 feet
                    GPS: Not Available

DIRECTIONS: [YAKIMA] From Yakima, travel south on Highway 82 for about 3 miles to the Union Gap exit. At the bottom of the off ramp, take a right and then a left at the first stop light. Continue on and at the next stop light take a right. Follow this road approximately 19 miles to the small town of Tampico and bear right. Keep going and just a little ways past the Ahtanum Meadows campground you want to bear right onto the North Fork Road. Follow this and in about 2.4 miles you arrive at the campground on your left.

COMMENTS: Another forested campground situated on Ahtanum Creek. This is one of many beautiful spots in the area and just recently re-opened. Snow Cabin Campground, in the Ahtanum State Forest, has a small creek running near it and offers a secluded camping stay.
Discover Pass

DISPERSED CAMPS

FOREST ROAD 2329

From Trout Lake, travel north on the Mt. Adams Recreational Highway, for about 1.5 miles and at the junction with forest roads #23 and #80, bear left onto forest road #23. Continue on this road until you come to the junction with forest road #90. At this point you want to stay on road #23 which soon turns to gravel. After passing the road for Council Lake, continue on and at the junction with roads 5601 and 2329 take road 2329. There are a couple of nice sites before arriving at Killen Creek campground.

FOREST ROAD 5603

Continuing on forest road 2329 past Killen Creek, Keenes, and Horseshoe Campgrounds, which are not only no longer free but extravagantly priced, you will come to forest road 5603. Take a left here onto the pavement. The road will go to gravel after awhile and there are some nice dispersed sites to be found.

CISPUS RIVER

From Randle, travel south on Forest Service Road # 25 and at the junction with Forest Service Road #23 bear left onto # 23. This is the Cispus River Road. This road leads you into the back country and there are some nice dispersed sites along the way including a beautiful site on the left side of the road right before you arrive at Adams Fork Campground.

ADAMS ROAD 239 DRAIN

From Quincy, travel south on highway 281 for about 4.5 miles and take a right at 5th N.W. There is a golf course at that corner. Follow this road for about 1.5 miles where you'll see a sign on the left. I believe it's a wildlife sign. Follow this road down and you'll come to a lake that is day use only. Follow the road around to the right and you find many open camp sites, some vault toilets are available. There are many campsites here most without shade but continuing on there is one site alone in the trees with a nice place to swim. You have to be lucky to get this one.

SUMMIT CREEK DISPERSED

From Glenwood, travel east on Highway 142 past the Klickitat Fish Hatchery on the left, and at a wide gravel road, take a left. Continue on this road and just past the 3 mile mark there are 2 dispersed sites on the right side of the road. These 2 dispersed campsites set on the creek in forest setting. There are no tables or toilets.

FRENCH CABIN CREEK RECREATION AREA

From Cle Elum, WA follow Highway 903 N and Salmon La Sac Road about 15.5 miles to Forest Road 4308. Turn left onto Forest Road 4308 and continue another .5 miles. Site will be on the left. This dispersed camping area is located along the west bank of the Cle Elum River north of Cle Elum Lake. You'll find a toilet but no tables.

HALFWAY SPRINGS DISPERSED

From Entiat, travel south on US-97A for 1.2 miles and take a right, west, onto the Entiat River Road. Continue on this road for about 28.5 miles, and take another right onto Forest Service Road 5900, the Shady Pass Road. Follow this road for about 6 miles to the site. This site offers 4 tent only sites. Trailers are not recommended.

BIG HILL CAMPSITE

From Entiat, travel south on US-97A for 1.2 miles and take a right, west, onto the Entiat River Road. Continue on this road for about 28.5 miles and take another right onto Forest Service Road 5900, the Shady Pass Road, and stay on 5900 for about 8 miles. Turn left on Forest Spur Road 112 and travel about 3 miles to the end of road. The road in to this rustic dispersed site is very rough and trailers are not advised. There is a toilet and shelter on site.

LONGMIRE MEADOW

From Naches, travel west on Highway 12 for about 4.4 miles and continue straight onto Highway 410 west for about 24.2 miles. At this point, take a right onto the Little Naches Road, Forest Service Road 19 and follow for another 4 miles. The site is on the right side of the road. This is a Popular OHV staging area with motorcycle trails nearby. If you're not into dirt bikes this may not be the place for you. Toilets are available.

LOST LAKE CAMPING AREA

From Naches, travel west on Highway 12 for about 22 miles and take a left onto Forest Service Road 1200, the Tieton Reservoir Rd. Follow this road for about ¼ mile to Forest Service Road 1201 and take a left. Continue on approximately 4 miles to the entrance on the left side on Forest Service Road 562. Set next to Lost Lake, this area offers dispersed camping with limited space. No amenities, Self-service. This is a popular fishing spot in the spring.

Northeast Region

Includes Counties:

Douglas
Ferry
Lincoln
Okanogan
Pend Oreille
Spokane
Stevens

BOULDER CREEK/SHREW   (WINTHROP)

Number of sites: 20   Type: tents; small trailers
Toilets: yes   Setting: forest; creek
Tables: no   Fire: fire rings
Fishing: yes   Hiking: yes
Handicap Access: no   Elevation: 2200 feet
          GPS: Lat: 48.57900173   Long: -120.1744863

DIRECTIONS: [OKANOGAN] On entering the town of Winthrop from the west, take a left at the 4 way stop and follow this road around to the right. This is the East Chewuch Road. Follow this road for about 5.8 miles and take a right onto the Boulder Creek Road, Forest Service Road 37. Continue on this road for about .5 miles and take a left into the large camp. There is no sign on the road, so heads up!

COMMENTS: This is a very large campground with sites going off in all directions including some set right on the river. You can do some exploring to find the one just right for you. There are 2 toilets; one as you enter the campground and the other one is around to the right. The camp is set up for tents and trailers. There are sites in both shade and full sun.
Discover Pass

> *"It always rains on tents. Rainstorms will travel thousands of miles, against prevailing winds for the opportunity to rain on a tent."*
>
> *~Dave Barry*

LOWER BOBCAT (WINTHROP)

Number of sites: 20
Toilets: yes
Tables: no
Fishing: yes
Handicap Access: no

Type: tents; trailers
Setting: forest; creek
Fire: fire rings
Hiking: yes
Elevation: 2220 feet

GPS: Lat: 48.6113865   Long: -120.1664302

DIRECTIONS: [OKANOGAN] On entering the town of Winthrop from the west, take a left at the 4 way stop and follow this road around to the right. This is the East Chewuch Road. Follow this road for about 5.9 miles and at the junction go right. Continue on this road, the Chewuch River Road, for about 3.6 miles to the camp on the right. There's a sign on the road that says Public Hunting. This is where you make your turn.

COMMENTS: This campground has room for maybe 15-20 campers, with about 10 sites set back in the woods and the others in meadow. There are vault toilets and fire rings but no tables. **Discover Pass**

UPPER BOBCAT (WINTHROP)

Number of sites: 35
Toilets: yes
Tables: no
Fishing: yes
Handicap Access: yes

Type: tents; trailers
Setting: forest; creek
Fire: fire rings
Hiking: yes
Elevation: 2230 feet

GPS: Lat: 48.6310632   Long: -120.1590989

DIRECTIONS: [OKANOGAN] On entering the town of Winthrop from the west, take a left at the 4 way stop and follow this road around to the right. This is the East Chewuch Road. Follow this road for about 5.9 miles and at the junction go right. Continue on this road, the Chewuch River Road, for about 5 miles and take a right at the public hunting sign on the right side of the road.

COMMENTS: This is another very large campground with enough spots for 35 or so camps. There are accessible toilets and fire rings but no tables. The sites are spread out nicely for privacy. The sites at the entrance to this camp are set in meadow. There's room enough here for larger trailers and motor homes as well as tents. **Discover Pass**

TIFFANY SPRING

Number of sites: 6
Toilets: yes
Tables: yes
Fishing: yes
Handicap Access: no

Type: tents
Setting: forest; creek
Fire: fire grates
Hiking: yes
Elevation: 6800 feet

GPS: Lat: 48.70054 Long: -119.95406

DIRECTIONS: [OKANOGAN] upon entering the town of Winthrop from the west, take a left at the 4 way stop and follow this road around to the right. This is the East Chewuch Road. Follow this road for about 5.8 miles and take a right onto the Boulder Creek Road, Forest Service Road 37. Continue on this road for 7.5 miles to a "Y", and bear left. Follow this road another 5.5 miles and bear left onto Forest Service Road 39. Keep going another 7.2 miles to the campground on your right.

COMMENTS: This campground is set at 6800 feet so don't expect to get here too early in the year. A trail leaves the campground taking you to Tiffany Lake, about a mile hike. From the lake, the trail branches out in all directions. **Note:** About 1.3 miles before arriving at Tiffany Spring, you come to North Fork Boulder Creek. There is a site with a picnic table and fire ring. This site is set right on the creek. And about .7 miles past Tiffany Spring is Parachute Meadow. This very large meadow is worth a visit.

BEAR CREEK (WINTHROP)

Number of sites: 25
Toilets: yes
Tables: no
Fishing: yes
Handicap Access: yes

Type: tents
Setting: forest; creek
Fire: rock fire rings
Hiking: yes
Elevation: 1800 feet

GPS: Lat: 48.4877158   Long: -120.1164504

DIRECTIONS: [OKANOGAN] From Winthrop, travel east on Highway 20 for about 14 miles through the town of Twisp and turn left onto the road signed for Davis Lake. Follow this road for about 7.6 mile and take a right onto the Bear Creek Road. In about 1.7 miles you'll come to a junction with the Bear Creek Road and Lester Road, stay straight on the Bear Creek Road. In another 1.8 miles bear right at the "Y" heading towards Cougar Lake. Follow this road for .7 miles to the campground set on both sides of the road.

COMMENTS: This campground is set in a pine forest with Bear Creek nearby. A couple of the sites are set on the creek. The campsites are for the most part large and private. Across the road on the left side coming in io a cito designated for handicapped persons. **Discover Pass**

RAMSEY CREEK   (WINTHROP)

Number of sites: 10
Toilets: yes
Tables: no
Fishing: yes
Handicap Access: yes

Type: tents
Setting: forest; creek
Fire: rock fire rings
Hiking: yes
Elevation: 1950 feet

GPS: Lat: 48.54226636 Long: -120.1452431

DIRECTIONS: [OKANOGAN] From Winthrop, travel east on Highway 20 for about 14 miles through the town of Twisp and turn left onto the road signed for Davis Lake. Follow this road for about 7.6 mile and take a right onto the Bear Creek Road. In about 1.7 miles you'll come to a junction with the Bear Creek Road and Lester Road. Stay straight on the Bear Creek Road. In another 1.8 miles bear left at the "Y" and follow this road for about 1.7 miles and take a left onto the Forest Service Road 200. Continue on for .2 miles and bear left onto Forest Service Road 215. In about 1 mile, you'll arrive at the site.

COMMENTS: This remote and very quiet camping area is set in a beautiful pine forest where many deer visit. The creek usually runs dry late into the summer. If you continue on Forest Service Road 215 a little further you'll come to another campsite with an outhouse.
Discover Pass

TWISP RIVER HORSECAMP   (WINTHROP)

Number of sites: 12
Toilets: yes
Tables: yes
Fishing: yes
Handicap Access: no

Type: tents; small trailers
Setting: forest; river
Fire: fire grates
Hiking: yes
Elevation: 3000 feet

GPS: Lat: 48.435582   Long: -120.529689

DIRECTIONS: [OKANOGAN] From Winthrop, travel east on Highway 20 for about 11 miles to the town of Twisp. At the Twisp River Road take a right and follow this for about 18 miles to the junction with Forest Service Road 4435 and bear left. In another 150 feet or so the pavement ends. Continue on, over the bridge, and then take a right. Follow this road another 3.5 miles to the campground.

COMMENTS: The 12 tree shaded campsites are designated for stock users/campers. There are hitch rails and feed stations along with a loading ramp in the campground located near Lake Chelan-Sawtooth Wilderness. Several trailheads are close by for hiking and horse riding. **NWFP**

BEAVER CREEK   (TWISP)

Number of sites: 15
Toilets: yes
Tables: yes
Fishing: yes
Handicap Access: yes

Type: tents; small trailers
Setting: forest; creek
Fire: fire grates
Hiking: yes
Elevation: 2700 feet

GPS: Lat: 48.43297675   Long: -120.0260763

DIRECTIONS: [OKANOGAN]   From Twisp, travel east on Highway 20 for approximately 2.3 miles to the junction with Highway 20 going east towards Okanogan. Take a left here and continue on for another 2.3 miles to the Upper Beaver Creek Road and take another left. Follow this road for 6.3 miles to the campground on your right.

COMMENTS: This is a large campground with spacious sites situated on a fast moving creek in a pine forest. Great hiking and mountain bike trails. **Discover Pass**

Number of sites: 12
Toilets: yes
Tables: no
Fishing: yes
Handicap Access: no

Type: tents
Setting: forest; meadow; lake
Fire: rock fire rings
Hiking: yes
Elevation: 3200 feet

GPS: Lat: 48.47651949 Long: -120.0960195

DIRECTIONS: [OKANOGAN] From Twisp, travel east on Highway 20 for 2.3 miles to the junction with Highway 20 going east towards Okanogan. Take a left here and continue on for another 2.3 miles to the Upper Beaver Creek Road and take another left. Follow this road another 6.3 miles to the Lester Road and take a left. Continue on for another 3.5 mile where you will come to a "Y" and bear right. Follow this road and then take the second road that goes to the right. In .8 miles you come to a "Y" and bear left. Continue on to the camping area on both sides of the road.

COMMENTS: This site is located in a large grassy meadow in a pine forest. If you can live without a picnic table this one may be for you. Just another .5 miles down the road, take a right and you come to Cougar Lake. There are also a couple of campsites here. Vault toilet, and fire rings. This is another good lake for canoes and small boats.
Discover Pass

We don't stop hiking because we grow old, we grow old because we stop hiking"

~Finis Mitchell

SPORTSMAN'S CAMP

Number of sites: 5
Toilets: yes
Tables: yes
Fishing: yes
Handicap Access: yes

Type: tents; small trailers
Setting: forest; creek
Fire: fire grates
Hiking: yes
Elevation: 2300 feet

GPS: Lat: 48.3912   Long: -119.8078

DIRECTIONS: [OKANOGAN]   From Twisp, travel east on Highway 20 for 2.3 miles to the junction with Highway 20 going east towards Okanogan. Take a left here and continue on for another 11.5 miles and turn left onto the Sweat Creek Road. There is no sign on the highway for Sweat Creek Road so after passing milepost 218, take the second left. This is Sweat Creek Road. Follow this road for about 1 mile to the campground entrance on your right.

COMMENTS: From the ATV-accessible forest roads to the quiet of nature back at the campground, this small campground in the Loup Loup Forest has something for everyone. A small stream flows along the edge of the campground. **Discover Pass**

ROCK CREEK

Number of sites: 4
Toilets: yes
Tables: yes
Fishing: yes
Handicap Access: yes

Type: tents
Setting: forest; creek
Fire: fire grates
Hiking: yes
Elevation: 2450 feet

GPS: Lat: 48.40626   Long: -119.7589534

DIRECTIONS: [OKANOGAN] From Twisp, travel east on Highway 20 for 2.3 miles to the junction with Highway 20 going east to Okanogan. Take a left here and travel approximately 16 miles to the Rock Creek campground turn off on your left. Follow this entrance road about 100 feet or so to a "T" and turn left. Follow this road 4 miles to the campground on your left.

COMMENTS: This is another campground set in a pine forest with meadows nearby. Just up the road a little is a very nice day use area with a large covered shelter and a vault toilet. **Discover Pass**

ROCK LAKES

Number of sites: 8
Toilets: yes
Tables: yes
Fishing: yes
Handicap Access: no

Type: tents
Setting: forest; lake
Fire: fire grates
Hiking: yes
Elevation: 3590 feet

GPS: Lat: 48.4526484   Long: -119.7886775

DIRECTIONS: [OKANOGAN]   From Twisp, travel east on Highway 20 for 2.3 miles to the junction with Highway 20 going east towards Okanogan. Take a left here and travel approximately 16 miles to the Rock Creek campground turn off on your left. Follow this entrance road about 100 feet or so to a "T" and turn left. Follow this road for about 9 miles to a "Y" and bear left. Continue on this road to the campground entrance on your left.

COMMENTS: This campground is well off the beaten path. It's a relaxing place with hiking, fishing, and swimming. There are trails from the campground leading to the two small lakes. **Discover Pass**

LEADER LAKE

Number of sites: 20
Toilets: yes
Tables: yes
Fishing: yes
Handicap Access: yes

Type: tents; small trailers
Setting: forest; lake
Fire: fire grates
Hiking: yes
Elevation: 2270 feet

GPS: Lat: 48.359898   Long: -119.696045

DIRECTIONS: [OKANOGAN] From Twisp, travel east on Highway 20 for 2.3 miles to the junction with Highway 20 going east towards Okanogan. Take a left here and travel approximately 17.5 miles and turn left at the campground entrance.

COMMENTS: Leader Lake Campground surrounds Leader Lake and offers boat launch facilities. A diverse population of spiny rays and rainbow trout makes this lake a favorite among local anglers. This is a larger campground than some of the others in the area. **Discover Pass**

PALMER LAKE (TONASKET)

Number of sites: 5
Toilets: yes
Tables: yes
Fishing: yes
Handicap Access: yes

Type: tents; small trailers
Setting: lake
Fire: fire grates
Hiking: no
Elevation: 1190 feet

GPS: Lat: 48.9159878   Long: -119.6342417

DIRECTIONS: [OKANOGAN] From Tonasket, travel north on Highway 97 for 6.5 miles to the Ellis Road and take a left. Follow this road for .5 miles where you will come to stop sign and take another left towards Loomis. In another 1.3 miles you'll come to another stop sign and this time you want to take a right. Continue on and in 11 miles arrive at the town of Loomis. Keep going through town and in 6.3 miles you come to Palmer Lake campground on your left.

COMMENTS: Located near Loomis, Palmer Lake Campground is near a 2,100-acre lake surrounded by orchards and mountainous terrain. It is a popular site for non-motorized boating. Site has seven campsites, vault toilet, and hand boat launch.
Discover pass

> *"It is entirely possible to spend your whole vacation on a winding mountain road behind a large motor home"*

CHOPAKA LAKE

Number of sites: 25
Toilets: yes
Tables: yes
Fishing: yes
Handicap Access: yes

Type: tents; small trailers
Setting: forest; lake
Fire: fire grates
Hiking: yes
Elevation: 2920 feet

GPS: Lat: 48.9140429 Long: -119.7022994

DIRECTIONS: [OKANOGAN] From Tonasket, travel north on Highway 97 for 6.5 miles to the Ellis Road and take a left. Follow this road for .5 miles where you will come to a stop sign and take a left towards Loomis. Follow this road and in 1.3 miles you'll come to another stop sign and this time you want to take a right. Continue on and in 11 miles you arrive at the town of Loomis. Keep going through town and in another 2.5 miles take a left onto the Toats Coulee Road. Follow this road for about 1.4 miles then take a sharp right up a steep hill. This is the Chopaka Grade Road. Continue on this road for about 3.4 miles and stay straight. Keep going for another 1.8 miles and bear right at the "Y". This will put you on the Forest Service Road 2400. Follow this road and in another 1.5 miles arrive at the lake. Follow road around to the left and into the campground.

COMMENTS: Primitive camping area located in northern Okanogan County, Chopaka Lake Campground is a popular fly-fishing site. Fishing and non-motorized boating on the lake. Numerous hiking trails explore the public lands north of the lake and also in the adjacent Loomis State Forest. Excellent wildlife watching for various waterfowl and for mountain goats on nearby Grandview Mountain. 4 of the sites have roofs over the tables. **Discover Pass**

TOATS COULEE

Number of sites: 6
Toilets: yes
Tables: yes
Fishing: yes
Handicap Access: no

Type: tents; small trailers
Setting: forest; creek
Fire: fire grates
Hiking: yes
Elevation: 3000 feet

GPS: Lat: 48.846   Long: -119.726

DIRECTIONS: [OKANOGAN] From Tonasket, travel north on Highway 97 for 6.5 miles to the Ellis Road and take a left. Follow this road for .5 miles where you will come to a stop sign and take a left towards Loomis. Follow this road and in 1.3 miles you'll come to another stop sign and this time you want to take a right. Continue on and in 11 miles you arrive at the town of Loomis. Keep going through town and in 2.5 miles take a left onto the Toats Coulee Road. Follow this road, which will turn into Forest Service Road 39, for about 5.5 miles to the campground entrance on your left.

COMMENTS: Toats Coulee Campground offers 6 sites. Glaciers and water have moved and smoothed giant boulders that make this campground unique. Campers can also enjoy a picnic near a forest stream. **Discover Pass**

UPPER TOATS COULEE

Number of sites: 4
Toilets: yes
Tables: yes
Fishing: yes
Handicap Access: no

Type: tents; small trailers
Setting: forest; creek
Fire: fire grates
Hiking: yes
Elevation: 3100 feet

GPS: Lat: Not available

DIRECTIONS: [OKANOGAN] From Toats Coulee campground, see above, travel .1 mile further to the campground on the left.

COMMENTS: This campground is also set on the Toats Coulee Creek. It is set in the forest with lots of shade. It's a very pretty campground. Fishing, hiking. **Discover Pass**

COLD SPRINGS (TONASKET)

Number of sites: 4
Toilets: yes
Tables: yes
Fishing: yes
Handicap Access: yes

Type: tents; small trailers
Setting: forest; creek
Fire: fire grates
Hiking: yes
Elevation: 6200 feet

GPS: Lat: 48.937   Long: -119.797

DIRECTIONS: [OKANOGAN]   From Tonasket, travel north on Highway 97 for 6.5 miles to the Ellis Road and take a left. Follow this road for .5 miles where you will come to a stop sign, and take another left towards Loomis. Follow this road for 1.3 miles to another stop sign and this time take a right. Continue on and in another 11 miles you come to the town of Loomis. Keep going through town and in 2.5 miles, take a left onto the Toats Coulee Road. Follow this road, which will turn into Forest Service Road 39, for about 7.7 miles and take a right at road signed Cold Springs campground, Forest Service Road 4000. In another .3 miles you come to a "Y" and you want to bear right. Continue on and in another 3.8 miles you come to another "Y" and this time bear left. Follow this road for 1.3 miles where you come to yet another "Y" and bear left again. Continue on for a little over a mile, and arrive at the campground on your left.

COMMENTS: At an elevation of 6,100 feet, Cold Springs Campground has views of the Pasayten Wilderness, Snowshoe Mountain, and Chopaka Mountain. Sites are surrounded by preserved land with more than 50 miles of trail. This is a wooded area with a creek and a picnic area. You may even get lucky and spot a Moose. **Discover Pass**

UPPER COLD SPRINGS (TONASKET)

Number of sites: 5
Toilets: yes
Tables: yes
Fishing: no
Handicap Access: no

Type: tents; small trailers
Setting: forest; creek
Fire: fire grates
Hiking: yes
Elevation: 6500 feet

GPS: Lat: Not available

DIRECTIONS: [OKANOGAN] From Cold Springs Campground, (above) travel another .4 miles, past the picnic area sign then stay to the right on the one-way campground road.

COMMENTS: There are 3 sites on this road, 2 on the right and one on the left. The 1st one on the right has a table and fire grate. The other 2 have only fire rings. There are toilets here as well. Keep going and bear right and at the end of the road there is another site off in the trees to the left with table and fire grate and then another site on the hill to the right with table and fire grate. Between the two is an accessible toilet.
Discover Pass

NORTH FORK NINE MILE (TONASKET)

Number of sites: 10
Toilets: yes
Tables: yes
Fishing: yes
Handicap Access: no

Type: tents; small trailers
Setting: forest; creek
Fire: fire grates
Hiking: yes
Elevation: 3500 feet

GPS: Lat: 48.8668186   Long: -119.7700784

DIRECTIONS: [OKANOGAN] From Tonasket, travel north on Highway 97 for 6.5 miles to the Ellis Road and take a left. Follow this road for .5 miles where you will come to a stop sign, and take another left towards Loomis. Follow this road for 1.3 miles to another stop sign and this time take a right. Continue on and in another 11 miles you come to the town of Loomis. Keep going through town and in 2.5 miles take a left onto the Toats Coulee Road. Follow this road, which will turn into the Forest Service Road 39, for about 8 miles to the campground on your right.

COMMENTS: This campground offers a forest setting on the North Fork Toats Creek. It is one of seven campgrounds in the vicinity. A trail leaves the site to a viewpoint. **Discover Pass**

LONG SWAMP (TONASKET)

Number of sites: 3
Toilets: yes
Tables: yes
Fishing: no
Handicap Access: no

Type: tents; small trailers
Setting: forest
Fire: fire grates
Hiking: yes
Elevation: 5500 feet

GPS: Lat: 48.85517 Long: -119.9462

DIRECTIONS: [OKANOGAN] From Tonasket, travel north on Highway 97 for 6.5 miles to the Ellis Road and take a left. Follow this road for .5 miles where you will come to a stop sign, and take another left towards Loomis. Follow this road for 1.3 miles to another stop sign and this time take a right. Continue on and in 11 miles you come to the town of Loomis. Keep going through town and in 2.5 miles take a left onto the Toats Coulee Road. Follow this road, which turns into Forest Service Road 39, for about 14 miles to the campground on your right. **Note:** just after you pass the Iron Gate trailhead road on your right, the campground is the next right after passing over cattle guard.

COMMENTS: This campground is right off of the road in a wooded area with lots of grass to lounge in. The 2 campsites and a corral on a creek in this small campground are mostly used by stock users. Located near Pasayten Wilderness the site has a hiking/horse riding trail access very close to the campground. **NWFP**

CRAWFISH LAKE   (OKANOGAN)

Number of sites: 16
Toilets: yes
Tables: yes
Fishing: yes
Handicap Access: yes

Type: tents; small trailers
Setting: mountain; lake
Fire: fire grates
Hiking: yes
Elevation: 4500 feet

GPS: Lat: 48.48376   Long: -119.21458

DIRECTIONS: [OKANOGAN] From the town of Okanogan, travel east on Highway 20 for approximately 11 miles to the turn off for the town of Riverside and turn right. Continue on through town and in about .5 miles, turn right on the Tunk Valley Road, go over the bridge and continue on for another .3 miles to a "T" where you want to take a left. Continue on for another 1.7 miles and bear right. Follow this road, where in about 13.5 miles the pavement ends. Continue on for another 4 miles, bear right at the "Y" and then go another 1 mile to the campground entrance on your left.

COMMENTS 16 rustic campsites and 1 picnic area are located on the northeast shore of the lake in a forested area. There is also a small group campsite. Activities include fishing, motor and non-motor boating, and picnicking. The southern and western shorelines are on the Colville Indian Reservation.

"State parks—that's where there are more things that you can't do than you can do"

136

FORDE LAKE (OMAK)

Number of sites: 8
Toilets: yes
Tables: no
Fishing: yes
Handicap Access: no

Type: tents
Setting: forest; lake
Fire: fire grates
Hiking: yes
Elevation: 1560 feet

GPS: Lat: 48.73692095 Long: -119.6700521

DIRECTIONS: [OKANOGAN] From Omak, travel east to the junction with Highways 20, 97 and 155 and go left following Highways 20/97 east. Continue on for about 12 miles past the small town of Riverside and taking a left onto the Pine Creek Road. Keep going on this road and in about 4.5 miles you'll come to a junction with North Pine Creek Road going right. You want to stay going straight. Continue on past Fish Lake and onto the Sinlahekin Road and go another 7 miles where you'll see the lake on the right and the campground on the left.

COMMENTS: This campground sets above Reflection Pond. Then in another 1/4 mile down the road you can take a left onto the reflection pond road where there is one site that sets above the pond. There is a rock fire ring but no table or toilet, but just a short distance away are the facilities for Forde Lake and toilets. **Discover Pass**

CONNER LAKE   (OMAK)

Number of sites: 3   Type: tents
Toilets: yes   Setting: forest; lake
Tables: no   Fire: fire grates
Fishing: yes   Hiking: yes
Handicap Access: no   Elevation: 1500 feet
        GPS: Lat: 48.02277393 Long: -122.0344958

DIRECTIONS: [OKANGAN] From Omak, travel east to the junction with Highways 20, 97 and 155 and go left following Highways 20/97 east. Continue on for about 12 miles past the small town of Riverside and taking a left onto the Pine Creek Road. Keep going on this road and in about 4.5 miles you'll come to a junction with North Pine Creek Road going right. You want to stay going straight. Continue on past Fish Lake and onto the Sinlahekin Road and go another 8.5 miles and take a hairpin right turn then stay right at the "Y" and down to the lake.

COMMENTS: There are 2 sites on the right side in full sun as you enter the campground with an accessible toilet on the left. If you follow the gravel road around to the left you'll find another 1 site that's more private. All 3 sites have rock fire rings but no tables. Looks like room for tents only. **Discover Pass**

SINLAHEKIN CREEK   (OMAK)

Number of sites: 20
Toilets: yes
Tables: no
Fishing: yes
Handicap Access: no

Type: tents; small trailers
Setting: forest; creek
Fire: fire rings
Hiking: yes
Elevation: 1550 feet

GPS: Lat: 48.6926   Long: -119.695

DIRECTIONS: [OKANGAN] From Omak, travel east to the junction with Highways 20, 97 and 155 and go left following Highways 20/97 east. Continue on for about 12 miles past the small town of Riverside and taking a left onto the Pine Creek Road. Keep going on this road and in about 4.5 miles you'll come to a junction with North Pine Creek Road going right. You want to stay going straight. Continue on past Fish Lake and onto the Sinlahekin Road and go another 4.3 miles and take a left into the campground.

COMMENTS: This is a wide open campground set in a stand of Ponderosa Pine. There are at least 20 good campsites here with a few on Sinlahekin Creek which was low on water when I visited in September. There is room here for tents and trailers. **Discover Pass**

BLUE LAKE (OMAK)

Number of sites: 25
Toilets: yes
Tables: no
Fishing: yes
Handicap Access: yes

Type: tents; small trailers
Setting: forest; lake
Fire: fire rings
Hiking: yes
Elevation: 1685 feet

GPS: Lat: 48.6713176 Long: -119.689334

DIRECTIONS: [OKANGAN] From Omak, travel east to the junction with Highways 20, 97 and 155 and go left following Highways 20/97 east. Continue on for about 12 miles past the small town of Riverside and taking a left onto the Pine Creek Road. Keep going on this road and in about 4.5 miles you'll come to a junction with North Pine Creek Road going right. You want to stay going straight. Continue on past Fish Lake and onto the Sinlahekin Road and go another 3 miles and take a left into the campground.

COMMENTS: There are 4 sites at this entrance with accessible toilet and rock fire rings. Two of the sites offer a little shade with the other 2 in full sun. The boat launch is very steep. Blue Lake has three entrances with a combined 25 or so spots. The second 2 entrances offer more accessible toilets with both fire grates and rock fire rings but no tables. Many of the campsites set on or close to this nice size lake with Aspen and Ponderosa Pines in abundance. This is another good lake for a canoe or kayak. **Discover Pass**

FISH LAKE

Number of sites: 35
Toilets: yes
Tables: no
Fishing: yes
Handicap Access: yes

Type: tents; small trailers
Setting: forest; lake
Fire: fire rings
Hiking: yes
Elevation: 1590 feet

GPS: Lat: 48.6125571   Long: -119.7059835

DIRECTIONS: [OKANGAN] From Omak, travel east to the junction with Highways 20, 97 and 155 and go left following Highways 20/97 east. Continue on for about 12 miles past the small town of Riverside and taking a left onto the Pine Creek Road. Keep going on this road and in about 4.5 miles you'll come to a junction with North Pine Creek Road going right. You want to stay going straight. From this point it's another 3 miles and a left into the campground.

COMMENTS: There are 4 sites at this spot with accessible toilet and rock fire rings but no tables. But the best is yet to come. Follow the entrance road around to the left and then bear right which will take you to the other side of the lake. Here you will find another 35 or so sites with 3 more accessible toilets and fire rings but again, no tables. Many of the sites are set close to the lake with others in full sun. This is a good spot to bring your canoe or kayak. Campground will accommodate both tents and trailers. Following this road to the end will take you back to the Pine Creek Road but is now the gravel Sinlahekin Road. **Discover Pass**

NO NAME (OMAK)

Number of sites: 8
Toilets: yes
Tables: no
Fishing: yes
Handicap Access: no

Type: tents; small trailers
Setting: forest
Fire: fire rings
Hiking: yes
Elevation: 1550 feet

GPS: Lat: Not available

DIRECTIONS: [OKANGAN] From Omak, travel east to the junction with Highways 20, 97 and 155 and go left following Highways 20/97 east. Continue on for about 12 miles past the small town of Riverside and taking a left onto the Pine Creek Road. Keep going on this road and in about 4.5 miles you'll come to a junction with North Pine Creek Road going right. You want to stay going straight. Continue on past Fish Lake and onto the Sinlahekin Road and go another 1.3 miles and go right onto a dirt road.

COMMENTS: There are 8 sites here, some with fire grates and others with rock fire rings. There are toilets, but no tables. This is a little forest camp that is set close to the road. **Discover Pass**

GREEN LAKE (OMAK)

Number of sites: 10
Toilets: yes
Tables: yes
Fishing: yes
Handicap Access: no

Type: tents; small trailers
Setting: forest; lake
Fire: fire grates
Hiking: yes
Elevation: 1600 feet

GPS: Lat: 48.45122302   Long: -119.6271362

DIRECTIONS: [OKANGAN] From Omak, Take Highways 97/20 going towards Tonasket and make a left at the sign for Lake Conconully. Follow this road for about 4.5 miles and at the "T" you want to take a left. Continue on and in another .5 miles make a right onto the Green Lake Road. Follow this road, which soon turns gravel, and at 2.5 miles you'll come to Brown Lake with no facilities. Continue on for another mile and you arrive at Green Lake.

COMMENTS: This site features 2 vault toilets, tables, fire grates, a boat launch and about 10 private and shady sites, half of which set on the lake. Nice campground not too far from town. **Discover Pass**

ELL, ROUND, LONG LAKES

Number of sites: open
Toilets: yes
Tables: no
Fishing: yes
Handicap Access: no

Type: tents; small trailers
Setting: lake
Fire: rock fire rings
Hiking: no
Elevation: 2600 feet

GPS: Lat: 48.6016692 Long: -119.117932

DIRECTIONS: [OKANOGAN] From Tonasket, travel east on Highway 20 for 13 miles to the Aeneas Valley Road and take a right. Follow this road for another 7 miles or so to the lakes, all on your left and all within .5 miles of each other.

COMMENTS: I have bunched these 3 together because of their proximity to one another. There are no tables, but there are many sites in which to camp with fishing and swimming.

LYMAN LAKE

Number of sites: 4
Toilets: yes
Tables: yes
Fishing: yes
Handicap Access: no

Type: tents
Setting: forest; lake
Fire: fire grates
Hiking: yes
Elevation: 2900 feet

GPS: Lat: 48.52701 Long: -119.02122

DIRECTIONS: [OKANOGAN] from the town of Tonasket, travel east on Highway 20 for 13 miles to the Aeneas Valley Road and take a right. Follow this road for another 13 miles and then take another right onto the Lyman Lake, Moses Meadows Road. Continue on this road and then take another right about .3 miles after passing the National Forest boundary sign. From here it's about .3 miles to site.

COMMENTS: This campground sets on Lyman Lake in a forested area. Looks like a good place to spend a few days enjoying the quiet. There is fishing, swimming and bike riding.

THIRTEEN MILE   (TONASKET)

Number of sites: 4   Type: tents; small trailers
Toilets: yes   Setting: forest; river
Tables: yes   Fire: fire grates
Fishing: yes   Hiking: yes
Handicap Access: yes   Elevation: 2050 feet
           GPS: Lat: 48.481887 Long: -118.727262

DIRECTIONS: [FERRY] From Tonasket, travel east on Highway 20 for 41 miles to the town of Republic. At the stop sign at the entrance of town take a right and go another mile or so to the junction with Highways 20 and 21. Take a right onto Highway 21 and follow this road for 13 miles to campground entrance on your left, signed 13 mile trailhead.

COMMENTS: Four Dispersed tent or trailer sites at the Thirteen Mile Trail #23. Activities include hiking or horse riding and fishing the Sanpoil River. **NWFP**

LAMBERT FOREST CAMP   (REPUBLIC)

Number of sites: 5   Type: tents; small trailers
Toilets: yes   Setting: forest; creek
Tables: no   Fire: rock fire rings
Fishing: yes   Hiking: yes
Handicap Access: yes   Elevation: 3860 feet
           GPS: Lat: 48.72846111 Long: -118.5219444

DIRECTIONS: [FERRY] From Republic, travel north on Highway 21 for about 7 miles and take a right onto the Lambert Creek Road. Follow this road another 7.5 miles to the campground.

COMMENTS: 5 campsites are next to Lambert Creek and across from the Old Stage Trail #1 and Midnight Ridge Trailheads. Camping area has room for horse trailers and is fenced in. There is also a watering trough on site. There are some nice tent spots off to your right. Set on Lambert Creek, this camp offers hiking and horseback riding trails that lead to a number of peaks in the area.

ANKENY # 1

Number of sites: 15
Toilets: yes
Tables: no
Fishing: yes
Handicap Access: no

Type: tents; small trailers
Setting: lake
Fire: fire grates
Hiking: no
Elevation: 1575 feet

GPS: Lat: 47.62770919   Long: -119.3297676

DIRECTIONS: [GRANT] From Coulee City, travel west on Highway 2 for about 5 miles and at the junction with Highway 17, take a right at the Public Access sign. Bear left at the "Y" and in about a mile you'll arrive at the camp. There are about 15 designated sites, some with shade and grassy areas for tents. Fire grates and a boat launch but no tables and 1 vault toilet. This campground will accommodate both Tents and trailers.

COMMENTS: This camp is set at the south end of Banks Lake. The boat launch is at the far end of the campground. Good access to the lake. **Discover Pass**

BARKER CANYON RECREATION AREA   (GRAND COULEE)

Number of sites: 10
Toilets: yes
Tables: no
Fishing: yes
Handicap Access: no

Type: tents; small trailers
Setting: lake, canyon
Fire: fire grates
Hiking: yes
Elevation: 1730 feet

GPS: Lat: 47.90261954   Long: -119.1690403

DIRECTIONS: [GRANT] From Grand Coulee, take Highway 174 west. Follow this highway for about 9.5 miles and take a left onto the Barker Canyon Road. Continue on this road for about 6 miles to the site.

COMMENTS: As you enter the site, the road to the left leads to a boat launch with a vault toilet. To the right are the campsites. There are about 10 of them, mostly set on the lake with some in shade. There are fire rings but no tables and the one toilet is at the boat launch. This site is set on the northwest end of Banks Lake with cliffs to your back and the lake in front. **Discover Pass**

LAKEVIEW RANCH CAMPGROUND   (ODESSA)

Number of sites: 4   Type: tents; small trailers
Toilets: yes   Setting: canyon
Tables: yes (1)   Fire: fire grates
Fishing: no   Hiking: yes
Handicap Access: yes   Elevation: 2300 feet
          GPS: Lat: 47.388479 Long: -118.721705

DIRECTIONS: [LINCOLN] From Odessa, Travel north on state route 21 for about 3 miles and take a left onto the Lakeview Ranch Loop Road. This is a gravel road. Follow this road for another 1.5 miles to the campground entrance on the right.

COMMENTS: There are 4 sites with 1 table, an accessible toilet and fire grates. Although the lake is now dry, the area boasts unique geological features such as the Odessa Craters area, 5 miles north of Odessa, Washington off Highway 21. There are a number of hiking trails in the area including the 12.5 mile Odessa to Pacific Lake Trail that winds through shrub-steppe uplands and the Lake Creek Canyon between the town of Odessa, Washington and Pacific Lake/Lakeview Ranch.

COFFEE POT LAKE CAMPGROUND   (ODESSA)

Number of sites: 6   Type: tents; small trailers
Toilets: yes   Setting: lake, canyon
Tables: yes   Fire: fire grates
Fishing: yes   Hiking: yes
Handicap Access: yes   Elevation: 1820 feet
          GPS: Lat: 47.500416 Long: -118.556567

DIRECTIONS: [LINCOLN] From Odessa, Travel north on state route 21 for about 6.5 miles where at the "Y" you want to bear right onto the Coffee Pot Road. Follow this road for 5.7 miles to the campground entrance road on the right.

COMMENTS: 6 sites all close together with a covered picnic site in a grassy area. All sites have tables and there is an accessible toilet on site. There's a boat launch and a small dock as well. All set in a beautiful canyon. Good canoe or Kayak lake.

TWIN LAKES CAMPGROUND   (ODESSA)

Number of sites: 3
Toilets: yes
Tables: yes
Fishing: yes
Handicap Access: yes

Type: tents; small trailers
Setting: lake, canyon
Fire: fire grates
Hiking: yes
Elevation: 1900 feet

GPS: Lat: 47.529749   Long: -118.505917

DIRECTIONS: [LINCOLN] From Odessa, Travel north on state route 21 for about 6.5 miles where at the "Y" you want to bear right onto the Coffee Pot Road. Follow this road for 6.8 miles and take a left onto the Highline Road. Continue on for another 1.5 miles to the campground entrance road on the right. From here it's a couple of miles down to the site.

COMMENTS: There are 3 sites on the left side as you enter the camp, all on grass with another lone site to the right on a knoll overlooking everything. All sites include tables, fire grates and there is an accessible toilet and a small boat launch. This is another wonderful lake for canoes and kayaks. **Note:** All three of these camps are located at or near the "Channeled Scablands" part of Eastern Washington, where Ice-Age floods carved deep canyons through the basalt. There are trails in the area.

BEAL PARK   (CURLEW)

Number of sites: 3
Toilets: yes
Tables: yes
Fishing: yes
Handicap Access: no

Type: tents; small trailers
Setting: river
Fire: fire grates
Hiking: yes
Elevation: 1850 feet

GPS: Lat: Not Available

DIRECTIONS: [FERRY] From Curlew, travel west on the West Kettle River Road for about 7.5 miles to the Beal Park camp on the right.

COMMENTS: This camp is set near the Kettle River and right off the highway with just a short walk to the water. All the sites are close together. This is a good place to park it for campers traveling east or west on the back roads of Northwest Washington.

147

LONE RANCH PARK (CURLEW)

Number of sites: 8
Toilets: yes
Tables: yes
Fishing: yes
Handicap Access: no

Type: tents; small trailers
Setting: forest; river
Fire: fire grates
Hiking: yes
Elevation: 1950 feet

GPS: Lat: Not Available

DIRECTIONS: From Curlew, travel north on Highway 21 for about 7.9 miles to the campground entrance on the right.

COMMENTS: (FERRY) This county park is about 4 miles south of the Canadian border. It is set on the Kettle River with hiking trails nearby. There is no sign on the highway for this one, so stay alert.

LITTLE CREEK (REPUBLIC)

Number of sites: 2
Toilets: yes
Tables: no
Fishing: yes
Handicap Access: yes

Type: tents
Setting: forest; creek
Fire: fire grates
Hiking: yes
Elevation: 4800 feet

GPS: Lat: Not Available

DIRECTIONS: [FERRY] From Republic, travel east on Highway 20 for about 8 miles to the Hall Creek Road and take a right. Follow this road for 3.3 miles where you will come to a junction and you want to stay straight on the main road. Continue on this road for about 1.3 miles and bear left at the "Y". In .8 miles you'll come to another "Y" and this time bear right. At 1.6 miles further on, you arrive at the campsite on your left.

COMMENTS: This camp is set in a forest meadow on a small creek. This is a very relaxing little spot with plenty of hiking trails nearby.

JUNGLE HILL TRAILHEAD   (REPUBLIC)

Number of sites: 5
Toilets: yes
Tables: yes
Fishing: no
Handicap Access: yes

Type: tents; small trailers
Setting: forest
Fire: fire grates
Hiking: yes
Elevation: 4300 feet

GPS: Lat: 48.63444   Long: -118.5505556

DIRECTIONS: [FERRY] At the stop sign at the entrance of the small town of Republic, take a right and go another mile or so to the junction with Highways 20 and 21. Take a left, and in just a little bit you'll come to another junction with Highway 21 going north and Highway 20 going east. Take Highway 20 east and travel on another 20.5 miles to the Albian Hill Road and take a left. Now on Forest Service Road 2030, continue on about a mile to a "Y" and bear left. Follow this road another 3.5 miles to the site.

COMMENTS: 5 developed campsites with 1 double campsite are found in this horse friendly campground near a stream. Loading ramp provided. Site is located at the trailhead. Also some dispersed campsites are outside of the campground. Jungle Hill Trail leads uphill to Kettle Crest Trail. Hiking and horse riding on the trail. Scenic driving on area roads.

WAPALOOSII   (REPUBLIC)

Number of sites: 5
Toilets: yes
Tables: yes
Fishing: no
Handicap Access: no

Type: tents
Setting: forest
Fire: fire grates
Hiking: yes
Elevation: 5000 feet

GPS: Lat: 48.66333   Long: -118.4383333

DIRECTIONS: [FERRY] From Republic, travel east on Highway 20 for approximately 20.5 miles and turn left onto the Albian Hill Road, Forest Service Road 2030. In .5 miles you want to bear right at the "Y" and continue on for 2.6 miles to the campground entrance.

COMMENTS: 5 campsites with tables are near the trailhead. Wapaloosie Trail connects to Kettle Crest Trail. Scenic views along the trail. Hiking, mountain biking, and horse riding on the trail. Scenic driving on Hwy 20.

149

STICKPIN (REPUBLIC)

STICKPIN (REPUBLIC)

Number of sites: 2
Toilets: no
Tables: yes
Fishing: no
Handicap Access: no

Type: tents
Setting: forest
Fire: fire grates
Hiking: yes
Elevation: 4250 feet

GPS: Lat: 48.7609, -118.4328

DIRECTIONS: [FERRY] From Republic, travel east on Highway 20 for approximately 20.5 miles and turn left onto the Albian Hill Road, Forest Service Road 2030. In .5 miles you want to bear right at the "Y" and continue on for 4.1 miles where you will come to the Old Stage Trailhead. From here, continue on straight for another 4.7 miles and bear left onto Forest Service Road 900. In .1 mile further you'll come to another junction and follow the road around to your left. In another .6 miles stay to the right and follow this road to the site.

COMMENTS: Another trailhead camp, this one has trails that will take you to many of the mountain peaks in the area. Hikers and horseback riders welcome. This camp is even more remote than Wapaloosii, so don't forget to bring lots of water.

TROUT LAKE (REPUBLIC)

Number of sites: 6
Toilets: yes
Tables: yes
Fishing: yes
Handicap Access: no

Type: tents
Setting: forest; creek; lake
Fire: fire grates
Hiking: yes
Elevation: 3050 feet

GPS: Lat: 48.62416667   Long: -118.23888

DIRECTIONS: [FERRY] From Republic, travel east to the junction with Highways 20 and 21. Take a left, and in just a little bit you'll come to another junction with Highway 21 going north and Highway 20 heading east. Take Highway 20 east for approximately 34 miles to the Trout Lake Road and take a left. Follow this road for 5 miles to the campground.

COMMENTS: This is a wonderful place. This campground is situated on Trout Lake. There is a creek that runs through the site and a trail that leads to Emerald Lake and Hoodoo Canyon. Activities include fly fishing only, non-motorized boating

DAVIS LAKE (REPUBLIC)

Number of sites: 7
Toilets: yes
Tables: yes
Fishing: yes
Handicap Access: yes

Type: tents; small trailers
Setting: mountain; lake
Fire: fire grates
Hiking: yes
Elevation: 4500 feet

GPS: Lat: 48.73860062   Long: -118.2286897

DIRECTIONS: [FERRY] From Republic, travel east to the junction with Highways 20 and 21. Take a left and in just a little bit you'll come to another junction with Highway 21 going north and Highway 20 heading east. Take Highway 20 heading east and travel about 40 miles to the junction with Highway 395. Take a left and follow this road for about 6 miles to the Deadman Creek Road and take a left here. Continue on this road for just over .5 miles to a "Y" and bear right. Follow this road for about 3 miles to the Jack Knife Lookout Road and take another right. Continue on for another 3 or so miles to a junction where you want to stay straight. Keep going another mile or so to a "Y" and bear left. Follow this road for another 5.3 miles to the campground entrance.

COMMENTS: This is another beautiful mountain lake. The road in can be rough in places but the good fishing makes the venture worth it. Set in beautiful forest with fishing, swimming and hiking around the lake.

SUMMIT LAKE

Number of sites: 6
Toilets: yes
Tables: yes
Fishing: yes
Handicap Access: no

Type: tents; small trailers
Setting: forest; creek
Fire: fire grates
Hiking: yes
Elevation: 2600 feet

GPS: Lat: 48.957858 Long: -118.126202

DIRECTIONS: [STEVENS] From Kettle Falls, travel west on Highway 395 crossing over the Columbia River Bridge then continuing north on Highway 395 for about 11.5 miles to the small town of Barstow. There is a small gas station and store on the right side of the highway. Take a right here, signed Pierre Lake, and travel another 1 mile again crossing over the Columbia River. At the stop sign, you want to take a left and follow this road for 10.2 miles and then bear right on road signed for Sheep Creek. Immediately take a left and follow this road for 2.5 miles to Forest Service Road 040 and take another left. Continue on down this road to the campground.

COMMENTS: What a great little find this was. The camp is set right on Summit Lake in a beautiful forested area. It's very secluded. Bring your canoe or kayak if you have one.

> *"Perhaps the truth depends on a walk around the lake."*
>
> *~Wallace Stevens*

ELBOW LAKE   (KETTLE FALLS)

Number of sites: 6   Type: tents; small trailers
Toilets: yes   Setting: forest; creek
Tables: yes   Fire: fire grates
Fishing: yes   Hiking: yes
Handicap Access: no   Elevation: 2775 feet
GPS: Lat: 48.948344   Long: -117.984224

DIRECTIONS: [STEVENS] From Kettle Falls, travel west on Highway 395 crossing over the Columbia River Bridge then continuing north on Highway 395 for about 11.5 miles to the small town of Barstow. There is a small gas station and store on the right side of the highway. Take a right here, signed Pierre Lake, and travel another 1 mile again crossing over the Columbia River. At the stop sign, you want to take a left and follow this road for 10.2 miles and then bear right on road signed for Sheep Creek. Bear right again and proceed for 1.4 miles where you want to bear right once again heading towards Sheep Creek and Northport. Follow this road for 8.3 miles and bear right onto Forest Service Road 15 heading towards Elbow Lake and Northport. Continue for 1.8 miles and take a right onto Forest Service Road 600 and follow this road for .5 miles to the campground.

COMMENTS: This is another remote and secluded camp set on a beautiful lake. The deep blue water makes me think that this lake is pretty deep. This is another good canoe lake. **Note:** After leaving Elbow Lake, continuing on Forest Service Road 15 will take you past Upper Sheep Creek dispersed and Sheep Creek campgrounds, then into the town of Northport.

SHEEP CREEK   (KETTLE FALLS)

Number of sites: 12
Toilets: yes
Tables: yes
Fishing: yes
Handicap Access: no

Type: tents; small trailers
Setting: forest; creek
Fire: fire grates
Hiking: yes
Elevation: 1570 feet

GPS: Lat: 48.960197   Long: -117.835536

DIRECTIONS: [STEVENS] From Kettle Falls, travel north on Highway 25 for approximately 35 miles to the town of Northport. Continue on through town and over the Columbia River Bridge. Follow his road for another mile to the Sheep Creek Road and take a left. Go straight up the gravel road, past the car race track, and in 4.5 miles arrive at the campground on your right.

Note: This campground was closed by The Department of Natural Resources because of budget cuts. The town of Northport has taken over the management of the campground so it is still free. This camp has always been one of my favorites in the state of Washington. Thank you town of Northport!

COMMENTS: This campground is oot on Sheep Creek a little northwest of the town of Northport. There are Lots of trees and lots of room. This is a good one for the family with a nice day use area. Hiking trails nearby. Just up the road about 1 mile is the Upper Sheep Creek dispersed camp with 2 campsites that set very close to the Creek. **Discover Pass**

DOUGLAS FALLS GRANGE PARK   (COLVILLE)

Number of sites: 6
Toilets: yes
Tables: yes
Fishing: yes
Handicap Access: yes

Type: tents; small trailers
Setting: forest; creek
Fire: fire grates
Hiking: yes
Elevation: 1825 feet

GPS: Lat: 48.616695   Long: -117.904509

DIRECTIONS: [STEVENS] From Colville, travel north on Highway 395 for a couple miles to junction with the Williams Lake Road and go right. Continue on this road for 4.5 miles to the Gillette Road and take another right. Now follow this road about .5 miles and bear right onto the Falls Road. Continue on another 1.5 miles to the campground on your right.

COMMENTS: This campground has it all. Besides the great day use shelter area, there is a nature trail and another trail that leads to a 60 foot high waterfall, and a baseball field. The campground is situated on 120 acres with a lot of space between the sites. **Discover Pass**

BIG MEADOW LAKE   (COLVILLE)

Number of sites: 6
Toilets: yes
Tables: yes
Fishing: yes
Handicap Access: no

Type: tents; small trailers
Setting: forest; creek
Fire: fire grates
Hiking: yes
Elevation: 3400 feet

GPS: Lat: 48.725745   Long: -117.56275

DIRECTIONS: [STEVENS] From Colville, travel east on Highway 20 for 1 mile to the Aladdin Road and take a left. Follow this road for about 20 miles to the Big Meadows Road and turn right. Continue on this road (gravel), another 6 or so miles to the campground.

COMMENTS: The campground is situated in a wooded area with meadows. Many of the sites are set right on the lake. There is a dock with benches for lake viewing along with fishing, hiking and swimming. Also boating and a boat launch. Interpretive trails.

STARVATION LAKE   (COLVILLE)

Number of sites: 6   Type: tents; small trailers
Toilets: yes   Setting: forest; creek
Tables: yes   Fire: fire grates
Fishing: yes   Hiking: yes
Handicap Access: no   Elevation: 2370 feet
     GPS: Lat: 48.493154   Long: -117.708474

DIRECTIONS: [STEVENS] From Colville, travel east on Highway 20 for about 10.5 miles to the Starvation Lake Road and take a right. In another .3 miles, go left at the fork in the road. From here it's another .5 miles to the campground on your right.

COMMENTS: This campground features lots of trees with open areas as well. Nice place to be on a hot summer day. Enjoy the fishing, swimming. There is a hand boat launch. **Discover Pass**

ROCKY LAKE   (COLVILLE)

Number of sites: 5   Type: tents; small trailers
Toilets: yes   Setting: forest; lake
Tables: yes   Fire: fire grates
Fishing: yes   Hiking: yes
Handicap Access: yes   Elevation: 2000 feet
     GPS: Lat: 48.496845   Long: -117.872200

DIRECTIONS: [STEVENS] From Colville at the junction of SR-20 and US Highway 395 travel east on State Route 20 for 5.9 miles and take a right onto the Artman-Gibson Road. Follow this road for 3.2 miles and take another right onto a one lane gravel road for .5 miles. Stay left and continue 2 miles to site.

COMMENTS: This small campground borders Rocky Lake, perfect for non-motorized boating, such as canoeing or lake kayaking. Fishing is catch-and-release only after June 1. **Discover Pass**

LITTLE TWIN LAKES   (COLVILLE)

Number of sites: 15   Type: tents; small trailers
Toilets: yes   Setting: forest; creek
Tables: yes   Fire: fire grates
Fishing: yes   Hiking: yes
Handicap Access: no   Elevation: 3700 feet
        GPS: Lat: 48.57416667 Long: -117.6441667

DIRECTIONS: [STEVENS] From Colville, travel east on Highway 20 for 12.5 miles to the Little Twin Lakes Road and take a left. Follow this road for 1.5 miles to a "Y" where you want to bear right. Continue on for another 3.5 miles and this time you want to bear left. Follow this road another .3 miles to the campground.

COMMENTS: 15 campsites set on both sides of the lake. Some campsites have great views of the lakes and wildlife. The Day-use area is good for viewing wildlife too. Boating both motor and non-motor, and fishing are popular. Nearby Radar Dome ORV Area is open to motor bikes & ATVs.

FLODELLE CREEK   (COLVILLE)

Number of sites: 6   Type: tents; small trailers
Toilets: yes   Setting: forest; creek
Tables: yes   Fire: fire grates
Fishing: yes   Hiking: yes
Handicap Access: no   Elevation: 3095 feet
        GPS: Lat: 48.545407 Long: -117.571006

DIRECTIONS: [STEVENS] From Colville, travel east on Highway 20 for about 19.5 to the Olson Creek Road and take a right. In about .3 miles bear left at the "Y" and in another .1 mile arrive at the campground.

COMMENTS: Camping near the Little Pend Oreille River, this one is situated on Flodelle Creek in a wooded area. Hiking and fishing. **Discover Pass**

SHERRY CREEK   (COLVILLE)

Number of sites: 6
Toilets: yes
Tables: yes
Fishing: yes
Handicap Access: no

Type: tents; small trailers
Setting: forest; creek
Fire: fire grates
Hiking: yes
Elevation: 2900 feet

GPS: Lat: 48.609136 Long: -117.54354

DIRECTIONS: [STEVENS] From Colville, travel east on Highway 20 for about 24 miles and turn right at the sign for Sherry Creek. Continue on for another .5 mile to campground. There is one site on the right before crossing bridge, 1 site on left after crossing bridge.

COMMENTS: This is a small wooded campground on Sherry Creek. There seems to be good fishing at the bridge. **Discover Pass**

CRESCENT LAKE RECREATION SITE   (METALINE FALLS)

Number of sites: 3
Toilets: yes
Tables: yes
Fishing: yes
Handicap Access: no

Type: tents; small trailers
Setting: forest; creek
Fire: fire grates
Hiking: yes
Elevation: 2000 feet

GPS: Lat: 48.9877778 Long: -117.31333

DIRECTIONS: From Metaline Falls, travel north on Highway 31 for about 12 miles and take a left onto Vista House Road, Forest Service Road 3165000. Continue on this road for about .25 miles to the campground entrance.

COMMENTS: This small lake offers 3 sites on the northwest side of Crescent Lake. Activities include fishing, boating and canoeing. This is a very beautiful area with many outdoor activities to explore. There is a rustic boat launch at the shore.

CANYON DAM (METALINE FALLS)

Number of sites: 6	Type: tents; small trailers
Toilets: yes	Setting: forest; creek
Tables: yes	Fire: fire grates
Fishing: yes	Hiking: yes
Handicap Access: no	Elevation: 2100 feet

GPS: Lat: 48.781448   Long: -117.418839

DIRECTIONS: [PEND OREILLE] From Metaline Falls, travel south on Highway 31 for 6.8 miles and turn left into Campbell Park.

COMMENTS: This is a great family camp spot. There is a roped off swimming area, a real nice lawn area where you can work on your tan, and an area to play volleyball.

SULLIVAN CREEK 1, 2, 3 (METALINE FALLS)

Number of sites: 6	Type: tents; small trailers
Toilets: yes	Setting: forest; creek
Tables: yes	Fire: fire grates
Fishing: yes	Hiking: yes
Handicap Access: no	Elevation: 2100 feet

GPS: Lat: Not Available

DIRECTIONS: [PEND OREILLE] Entering Metaline Falls, after crossing over the Pend Oreille River, bear left following Highway 31 for 2.2 miles and take a right at the Sullivan Lake Road, Forest Service Road 9345. Follow this road for 4.7 miles then take a left onto Forest Service Road 22. Continue on and in another 1.2 miles arrive at the first of the three sites.

COMMENTS: I've put all three of these camps together because they are all within a mile or so from each other and very much alike. Each camp has one creek side site and one across the road from the creek. Camp number 2 is about 1.3 miles further on and camp number 3 is .9 miles further yet. This is a very rugged area.

GYPSY MEADOWS   (METALINE FALLS)

Number of sites: 6   Type: tents; small trailers
Toilets: yes   Setting: forest; creek
Tables: yes   Fire: fire grates
Fishing: yes   Hiking: yes
Handicap Access: no   Elevation: 3500 feet
GPS: Lat: 48.903816   Long: -117.081349

DIRECTIONS: [PEND OREILLE] Entering Metaline Falls from the south, cross over Pend Oreille River Bridge and bear left. Follow this road for 2.2 miles and take a right at the Sullivan Lake Road, Forest Service Road 9345. Continue on this road for 4.7 miles and turn left onto Forest Service Road 22. Keep going on this road for 12 miles to the campground on your left.

COMMENTS: This campground has sites in the trees and there are also a few sites in the meadow. Straight across the entrance road is the Thunder Creek Trailhead. This is a very remote camp and probably gets little use. It's a very beautiful place. Oh, by the way, this area has been designated Grizzly Bear recovery habitat. Just thought you'd like to know.

> *"Hikers are warned to wear tiny bells on their clothing when hiking in bear country. The bells warn away MOST bears. Hikers are also cautioned to watch the ground on the trail, paying particular attention to bear droppings to be alert for the presence of Grizzly Bears. One can tell a Grizzly dropping because it has tiny bells in it"*

160

STAGGER INN CAMPGROUND   (METALINE FALLS)

Number of sites: 4
Toilets: yes
Tables: yes
Fishing: no
Handicap Access: no

Type: tents; small trailers
Setting: forest; creek; waterfall
Fire: fire grates
Hiking: yes
Elevation: 3290 feet

GPS: Lat: 48.7668667   Long: -117.0613417

DIRECTIONS: [PEND OREILLE] Entering Metaline Falls, cross over the Pend Oreille Bridge and bear left. Follow this road for 2.2 miles and take a right at the Sullivan Lake road, Forest Service Road 9345. Continue on this road for about 4.7 miles and at a junction you want to take Forest Service Road 22. Continue on this road for about 16 miles and stay going straight where Forest Service Road 22 turns into Forest Service Road 302. Follow this road for another 5.5 or so miles, to a "T" and go right. In about 1.5 miles you'll arrive at the camp on the right.

DIRECTIONS: FROM IDAHO: From the small town of Priest River, travel north on State Highway 57 for about 27 miles to the Reeder Bay Road and bear left onto Forest Service Road 302. Travel this road for about 20 miles to the site on the left. Although this campground is administered by the Panhandle National Forest of Idaho, it is located in Washington State.

COMMENTS: This is a great little campground set in an area that looks more like the Westside of the state. A short trail from the campground leads to scenic Granite Falls and the Roosevelt Grove of Ancient Cedars.

BATEY BOULD TRAILHEAD   (USK)

Number of sites: 6
Toilets: yes
Tables: yes
Fishing: yes
Handicap Access: no

Type: tents; small trailers
Setting: forest; creek
Fire: fire grates
Hiking: yes
Elevation: 2500 feet

GPS: Lat: 48.3711111   Long: -117.3722222

DIRECTIONS: [PEND OREILLE] From Usk, travel north on Highway 20 for approximately 4 miles to the Kirchan Road and take a left. Follow this road for about 1.5 miles where you will come to a "T" with a paved road. This is the west Calispell Road. Take a right and continue on for another 1 mile to the Sicely Road and take a left. Follow this road for 1.5 miles to the trailhead sign on your left.

COMMENTS: The campsites are all situated in a large meadow area. There are trailheads at the campground and just another 1 mile or so up the Sicely Road from the campground is Conger Lake on the left side of the road for fishing, hiking and swimming. **NWFP**

SKOOKUM CREEK   (USK)

Number of sites: 6
Toilets: yes
Tables: yes
Fishing: yes
Handicap Access: no

Type: tents; small trailers
Setting: forest; creek
Fire: fire grates
Hiking: yes
Elevation: 2040 feet

GPS: Lat: 48.3137939   Long: -117.2796637

DIRECTIONS: [PEND OREILLE] From Usk, travel east over the Pend Oreille River bridge and take a right on the Le Clerc Road. Follow this road for 3.3 miles to the Bear Park Road and take a left. Continue on this road for just a bit to the campground entrance then .3 miles to the site.

COMMENTS: 6 campsites and a picnic area with a day use shelter are situated on the South Fork of Skookum Creek. Abundant wildlife in the area. Fishing, and boating in the Pend Oreille River. **Discover Pass**

COOKS LAKE

Number of sites: 6
Toilets: yes
Tables: yes
Fishing: yes
Handicap Access: no

Type: tents; small trailers
Setting: forest; lake
Fire: fire grates
Hiking: yes
Elevation: 3075 feet

GPS: Lat: 48.343157 Long: -117.169295

DIRECTIONS: [PEND OREILLE] From Usk, travel east over the Pend Oreille River bridge and continue on straight following the road heading towards Browns Lake. In about 2 miles, take a right onto the Best Chance Road and follow this road until you come to a "Y" and bear right. Keep going another 3.3 miles to the campground.

COMMENTS: This Forest service campground has no toilets or tables. It is set right on Cooks Lake. Great for fishing, swimming, canoe and kayak.

MYSTIC LAKE

Number of sites: 6
Toilets: yes
Tables: yes
Fishing: yes
Handicap Access: no

Type: tents; small trailers
Setting: forest; creek
Fire: fire grates
Hiking: yes
Elevation: 3090 feet

GPS: Lat: Not Available

DIRECTIONS: [PEND OREILLE] From Usk, travel east over the Pend Oreille River bridge and continue on straight following the road heading towards Browns Lake. In about 2 miles take a right onto the Best Chance Road and follow this road until you come to a "Y" and bear right. Keep going another 5 miles or so to a "Y" and take a left. Follow this road another .3 miles to the campground entrance on your left.

COMMENTS: Another Forest Service campground with no toilets or tables. This is a very secluded camp in a wooded area with trails leading down to the lake.

NO NAME LAKE   (USK)

Number of sites: 6	Type: tents; small trailers
Toilets: yes	Setting: forest; creek
Tables: yes	Fire: fire grates
Fishing: yes	Hiking: yes
Handicap Access: no	Elevation: 4000 feet

GPS: Lat: 48.296580   Long: -117.132761

DIRECTIONS: [PEND OREILLE] From Usk, travel east over the Pend Oreille River bridge and continue on straight following the road heading towards Browns Lake. In about 2 miles take a right onto the Best Chance Road and follow this road until you come to a "Y" and bear right. Keep going another 5 miles or so to another "Y" and bear right towards Bead Lake. Continue on another 3.5 miles to the campground entrance on your left.

COMMENTS: Just before arriving at the campground, there are a couple of sites on your right. Keep going the best camping is just ahead. Forest setting with trails that lead to the lake. This is one of 3 rustic campgrounds within 10 miles. This camp offers Fishing and swimming.

FREEMAN LAKE   (USK)

Number of sites: 6   Type: tents; small trailers
Toilets: yes   Setting: forest; creek
Tables: yes   Fire: fire grates
Fishing: yes   Hiking: yes
Handicap Access: no   Elevation: 2475 feet
                GPS: Lat: Not Available

DIRECTIONS: [PEND OREILLE] From Usk, travel east over the Pend Oreille River bridge and continue on straight following the road heading towards Brown Lake. In about 2 miles take a right onto the Best Chance Road and follow this road until you come to a "Y" and bear right. Keep going another 5 miles or so to another "Y" and bear right towards Bead Lake. In .3 miles you'll come to another "Y" and you want to bear right. Continue on for another 8.5 miles to the Bench Road and take a left. Keep going for .8 miles where the pavement ends and go right. Follow this road for about a mile and take a left and then in .3 miles bear right at the "Y" and into the campground.

COMMENTS: Many good sites to choose from. The campground is situated on Freeman Lake with a very large meadow. There's lots of room to play, with fishing, swimming, canoe and kayak.

DRAGOON CREEK   (SPOKANE)

Number of sites: 20   Type: tents; small trailers
Toilets: yes   Setting: forest; creek
Tables: yes   Fire: fire grates
Fishing: yes   Hiking: no
Handicap Access: yes   Elevation: 1975 feet
        GPS: Lat: 47.88832   Long: -117.44314

DIRECTIONS: [Spokane] From Spokane, travel north on Highway 395 for 4 miles to the junction with Highway 2. Continue on Highway 395 for about 10.5 miles to the North Dragoon Creek Road and take a left. Follow this road for about .5 mile into the campground.

COMMENTS: This is a very large campground with sites both on and away from the creek. There is a large open day use area with a lot of grass. Good family campground not far from Spokane. **Discovery Pass**

DISPERSED CAMPS

MAZAMA DISPERSED

From the store in Mazama take road going towards Harts Pass. In about 6.5 miles the pavement ends then in another .3 miles starts a series of dispersed camps of the left side of the road. This is about a 1.5 mile stretch of road. There are probably 15-20 sites all together in the combined camps with a couple pretty close to the river. Then at the Robinson Creek bridge, on the right there is a nice site that sets right on the creek. It's close to the road but right on the water. There are also 2 other sites in the woods before you come to the Robinson Creek Trailhead parking area. There is a vault toilet at the trailhead and you need a trail pass to park there.

FOREST SERVICE ROAD # 37

Coming from Winthrop and just before arriving at the Chewuch River Road, turn right onto Forest Service Road # 37. Follow this road staying straight. In about 2 miles begins a series of dispersed sites on the right hand side of the road. Some of the spots set above the creek, some on the creek.

BOULDER CREEK BRIDGE SITES

Travel to the Boulder Creek/Shrew site, see campground listing above, and continue up Forest Service Road 37 for about 1/2 mile where you'll come to a bridge. On the left there is a steep little road leading to one site on the creek. Keep following this little dirt road and you'll come upon another 10 sites scattered throughout the forest, many close to the creek. At the end of the road there are a couple of large sites set close to the Chewuch with good swimming holes.

CHEWUCH RIVER ROAD

On entering Winthrop, take a left at the 4 way stop and follow this road for about 9 miles. You will come to a "T" and here you want to turn right. You are now on the Chewuch River Road. In about .8 miles you'll come to the small Forest Service Road # 015. Take a right down the hill to a dispersed site that sits above the river. There's a rock fire ring. About another 4.5 miles up the Chewuch River Road begins a series of dispersed sites on the river side of the road ending at the Andrews Creek

Trailhead site about 12 miles up the road. The first site is at Forest Service Road # 082. Do not attempt to enter this site with a trailer! There is no turn around and the entrance is pretty steep. You can probably get a small trailer into the rest of these sites. There are 13 dispersed sites including the Andrews Creek Trailhead site. Most have room for at least 2 camps; a couple are one camp sites, some with enough room for 3-4 camps. Some of the camps set above the river with trails leading to the water and others set on or close to the river. All sites require you to park and carry your gear a very short distance. There are rock fire rings but no tables or toilets except for the Andrews Creek site which has 2 tables and a vault toilet.

EASTSIDE CHEWUCH RIVER

Travel the Chewuch River Road and take a right onto Forest Service Road # 5110.As soon as you cross the bridge there is a nice dispersed spot on the left. Keep going and you'll want to bear right at the 1st and 2nd "Y". Continue on this road and in the next 8 miles begins a series of 11 mostly one site dispersed spots. Some of the sites require you to carry your gear a short distance but most you can drive to. There are a couple of sites with good beach access. These all have fire rings.

CONCONULLY DISPERSED SITE

From Conconully, take a right going towards Loomis. Continue on this road and at the north end of the lake there is a dispersed site with an outhouse. Good little site.

OROVILLE DISPERSED

From Oroville travelling towards Loomis on the Loomis Oroville Road, travel about 8 miles and on the left side of the road there is a small dirt road where you want to take a left. There is no sign so heads up. There are 4 sites here that set above the Similkameen River.

Another 2 miles further down the highway there is another dirt road on the left that leads to a dispersed site with about 10 sites that set all along the river with some shade.

SIDLEY LAKE

Just north of the old ghost town of Molson you come to Sidley Lake. The camping area sets on the lake. The first time I was here was in 1975 and we were the only people camping here. The last time I was here it was pretty much all trailers and motor homes lining the grass camping area. The good is that it's close to the old town of Molson with old buildings and museum.

UPPER SHEEP CREEK

After passing the Sheep Creek Campground, see Northeast Region, continuing another 1 mile there is a nice spot on the creek. Then in another .5 miles is the old Upper Sheep Creek camp. The toilet has been removed and now it's dispersed. There are a couple of sites here.

BEAR POT

From Republic, travel east on Highway 20 for about 8 miles to the Hall Creek Road and take a right. Follow this road for 3.3 miles where you will come to a junction and you want to stay straight on the main road. Continue on this road for about 1.3 miles and bear left at the "Y". In .8 miles you'll come to another "Y" and this time bear right. Follow this road for 1.2 miles to a "T" and turn left onto Forest Service Road 2054. Continue on for another .6 miles, bear left at the "Y" and follow this road, Forest Service Road 2055, for 3.6 miles to the campsite. This is truly a primitive camp spot. The site is used primarily by backpackers and horseman. There is no water in the area, so bring plenty. There is a trail that leads to Fire Mountain at 5890 feet.

COUGAR

From Republic, travel east on Highway 20 for about 8 miles to the Hall Creek Road and take a right. Follow this road for 3.3 miles where you will come to a junction and you want to stay straight on the main road. Continue on this road for about 1.3 miles and bear left at the "Y". In .8 miles you'll come to another "Y" and this time bear right. Follow this road for 1.2 miles to a "T" and turn left onto Forest Service Road 2054. Continue on for another .6 miles and bear right at the "Y" staying on Forest Service Road 2054. Follow this road for 2.8 miles and bear right at the "Y" and then continue on another 2 miles to the site. Another very remote spot, as with Bear Pot, this one is used primarily by backpackers and horseman. There is a trail heading east that leads to Thirteen Mile

Mountain at 4890 feet. The trail heading west leads to who knows where. Bring plenty of water.

BEAD LAKE BOAT LAUNCH

From Newport, follow U.S. Highway 2 across the Pend Oreille River into Idaho and turn north on LeClerc Road, County Road 9305. Continue on County Road 9305 for 2.8 miles and turn right onto the Bead Lake Road, County Road 3029. Follow this road for about 6 miles and turn right onto the Bead Lake Loop Road and continue for .2 miles to the turnoff for the boat launch. This boat launch provides public access to beautiful Bead Lake, 720 acres, which is the largest lake in Pend Oreille County. Parking is limited. The lake has four dispersed campsites located along the lakeshore which are accessed by either boat or hiking trail. The first campsite is a 1 mile hike, the next .5 miles further.

FISHTRAP RECREATION AREA

From Spokane, travel south on Interstate 90 for about 30 miles and take the 254 exit. Go left at the ramp and follow this road for about 1.75 miles to the public land access. This is a wide open dispersed camp setting. There are various habitat types from forest, shrub, grassland, wetlands and lakes. These areas are home to a wide variety of wildlife along with beautiful landscapes and even an old farmstead. Although there are no toilets at the site, some can be found close by.

Southeast Region

Source: diymaps.net (c)

Includes Counties:

Adams
Asotin
Benton
Columbia
Franklin
Garfield
Grant
Walla Walla
Whitman

SOUTHEAST REGION

COLUMBIA RIVER   (ELLENSBURG)

Number of sites: open
Toilets: yes
Tables: no
Fishing: yes
Handicap Access: no

Type: tents; small trailers
Setting: forest; creek
Fire: rock fire rings
Hiking: no
Elevation: 800 feet

GPS: Lat: Not Available

DIRECTIONS: [GRANT] From Ellensburg, travel east on Highway 90 for 28 miles and take the 137 exit heading towards Richland, Highways 26 and 243. In about a mile take Highway 243 toward Richland. Follow this road for another .5 mile and take a right into the camping area on your right.

COMMENTS: This wide-open camping area is set directly on the Columbia River. There is a fence at the entrance and some of the sites require a short walk-in. Other sites are drive to. This is a great location for folks that are attending music events at the Gorge Amphitheater.

BEVERLY DUNES   (ELLENSBURG)

Number of sites: open
Toilets: yes
Tables: no
Fishing: yes
Handicap Access: yes

Type: tents; small trailers
Setting: sand dunes; creek
Fire: rock fire rings
Hiking: yes
Elevation: 520 feet

GPS: Lat: Not Available

DIRECTIONS: [GRANT] From Ellensburg, travel east on Highway 90 for 28 miles and take the 137 exit heading towards Richland, Highways 26 and 243. In about a mile take Highway 243 towards Richland. Follow this road for about 7.2 miles and take a left onto Crab Creek Road. Continue on this road for another 2 miles to the site on your right.

COMMENTS: This site is used mainly by off road vehicle people. The campsites are set down in the trees not far from Crab Creek. Across Crab Creek Road is Nunnally Lake. **Discovery Pass**

LEWIS CREEK CAMP   (DAYTON)

Number of sites: 2   Type: tents
Toilets: yes   Setting: forest; creek
Tables: yes   Fire: fire grates
Fishing: yes   Hiking: yes
Handicap Access: no   Elevation: 4150 feet
                    GPS: Lat: Not Available

DIRECTIONS: [COLUMBIA] From Dayton, take a right on road number 9115, signed "ski". At some point this turns into Forest Service road 64. Follow this road for about 15 miles to the camp on the left.

COMMENTS: This is a private little camp with shade and creek access. Very secluded and peaceful.

TOUCHET CORRALS   (DAYTON)

Number of sites: 6   Type: tents; small trailers
Toilets: yes   Setting: forest; creek
Tables: yes   Fire. fire grates
Fishing: yes   Hiking: yes
Handicap Access: no   Elevation: 4230 feet
          GPS: Lat: 46.093261   Long: -117.847383

DIRECTIONS: [COLUMBIA] From Dayton, take a right on road number 9115, signed "ski". At some point this turns into Forest Service road 64. Follow this road for about 16 miles to the camp on the left.

COMMENTS: This camp is set in the forest on the Touchet River. This beautiful area offers plenty to do.

172

PATAHA CREEK (POMEROY)

Number of sites: 4
Toilets: yes
Tables: yes
Fishing: yes
Handicap Access: no

Type: tents; small trailers
Setting: forest; creek
Fire: fire grates
Hiking: yes
Elevation: 4000 feet

GPS: Lat: 46.29224 Long: -117.51387

DIRECTIONS: [GARFIELD] From the Pomeroy ranger station, travel east through town and turn right onto 15th street. Follow this road for about 7 miles to Mountain Road and take a left. The street sign for Mountain Road is after the actual turn, not before it, so "heads up". Continue on this road for another 1.5 miles, then cross a small bridge, and bear right at the "Y" onto the Pataha Creek Road. Follow this road for about 5.5 miles to the campground entrance on your left.

COMMENTS: What a nice spot. There is a small pond surrounded by meadow. Pataha Creek runs through the campground. It is situated in a pine forest off the beaten path, with hiking and fishing. Fish weirs have been installed to aid the passage of fish through a culvert in Pataha Creek. The creek is stocked each spring with fish.

BOUNDARY (POMEROY)

Number of sites: 5
Toilets: yes
Tables: yes
Fishing: no
Handicap Access: no

Type: tents; small trailers
Setting: forest
Fire: fire grates
Hiking: yes
Elevation: 4450 feet

GPS: Lat: 46.29272 Long: -117.5569

DIRECTIONS: [GARFIELD] From the Pomeroy Ranger station, head east through town and turn right onto 15th street. Follow this road for about 15.5 miles. At this point you enter the Umatilla National Forest. Look to your left and you will see the Boundary campground.

COMMENTS: This small campground has 5 tent or trailer campsites close to Wooten Wildlife Area. The campground is about 20 miles north of the Wehana-Tucannon Mountains Wilderness for hiking. Watch for wildlife in the area.

ALDER THICKET   (POMEROY)

Number of sites: 3   Type: tents; small trailers
Toilets: yes   Setting: forest
Tables: yes   Fire: fire grates
Fishing: no   Hiking: yes
Handicap Access: no   Elevation: 5100 feet
                GPS: Lat: 46.25917   Long: -117.56646

DIRECTIONS: [GARFIELD] From the Pomeroy Ranger station, head east through town and turn right onto 15th street. Follow this road for about 15.5 miles where the pavement ends, and continue on. In another 2.5 miles you come to a "Y" and you want to bear right. This is Forest Service Road 40. Continue on this road for another .5 miles to the campground on your right.

COMMENTS: This campground is located off of Forest Service Road 40, which is just three miles into the Blue Mountains. Overgrown trees and tall Alder shrubbery will provide plenty of shade for Grouse, White-Tailed deer and you on hot summer days.

> *"The tree which moves some to tears of joy is in the eyes of others only a green thing which stands in their way"*
>
> *~ William Blake*

BIG SPRINGS   (POMEROY)

Number of sites: 7   Type: tents; small trailers
Toilets: yes   Setting: forest; creek
Tables: yes   Fire: fire grates
Fishing: yes   Hiking: yes
Handicap Access: no   Elevation: 5000 feet
GPS: Lat: 46.22954   Long: -117.54279

DIRECTIONS: [GARFIELD] From the Pomeroy Ranger station, travel east through town and turn right onto 15th street. Follow this road for about 15.5 miles where the pavement ends, and continue on. In another 2.5 miles you come to a "Y" and you want to bear right. This is Forest Service Road 40. Continue on this road for another 5 miles where you come to the junction with Forest Service Road 42, and take a left. Notice the lookout tower to your right. Follow Forest Service Road 42 for 1 mile where you come to another junction and stay left. Continue on for about 2 miles to the campground entrance on your left and then bear left again on Forest Service Road 125 to the site.

COMMENTS: 7 tent or trailer camp sites are located north of the Wenaha-Tucannon Mountains Wilderness. This is the coolest campground during hot summer days. Hiking opportunities are in a close proximity of Big Springs. There are small trailer and tent sites, one vault toilet and a few picnic tables available for day use.

TEAL SPRING

Number of sites: 7
Toilets: yes
Tables: yes
Fishing: no
Handicap Access: no

Type: tents; small trailers
Setting: forest; mountain
Fire: fire grates
Hiking: yes
Elevation: 5600 feet

GPS: Lat: 46.190222   Long: -117.572189

DIRECTIONS: [GARFIELD] From the Pomeroy ranger station, travel east through town and turn right onto 15th street. Follow this road for about 15.5 miles to where the pavement ends, and continue on. In another 2.5 miles you come to a "Y" and you want to bear right. This is Forest Service Road 40. Continue on this road for another 5 miles where you come to a junction with Forest Service Road 42. There is a 100 foot lookout tower to your right. Follow Forest Service Road 40 going straight for about .5 miles to the campground entrance on your right, then another .5 miles to the site.

COMMENTS: 7 quaint campsites for tents and small trailers set on a ridge, offering a spectacular view of the Tucannon drainage and the Wenaha-Tucannon Wilderness. Many of the roads in the vicinity are popular with Off-Highway Vehicle enthusiasts and day-hike opportunities are available. Bear Creek Trailhead is close by. Other hiking opportunities are found in the nearby Wenaha-Tucannon Wilderness south of the campground.

.

Number of sites: 1   Type: tents
Toilets: yes   Setting: forest
Tables: yes   Fire: fire grate
Fishing: no   Hiking: yes
Handicap Access: no   Elevation: 4800 feet
                    GPS: Lat: Not Available

DIRECTIONS: [GARFIELD] From the Pomeroy Ranger station, follow Highway 12 east through town and turn right on 15th street. Follow this road for about 15.5 miles to where the pavement ends, and continue on. In another 2.5 miles, you come to a "Y" and you want to bear right. This is Forest Service Road 40. Continue on this road for another 5 miles where you come to a junction with Forest Service Road 42. Continue on Forest Service Road 40 for just over 3.5 miles and turn left on Forest Service Road 260. Follow this road into the campground.

COMMENTS: This very private campsite has enough room for maybe two vehicles. It's set in the forest with many hiking trails in the vicinity.

MISERY SPRINGS (POMEROY)

Number of sites: 5
Toilets: yes
Tables: yes
Fishing: no
Handicap Access: no

Type: tents
Setting: forest; mountain
Fire: fire grates
Hiking: yes
Elevation: 6000 feet

GPS: Lat: 47.751074 Long: -120.740139

DIRECTIONS: [GARFIELD] From the Pomeroy ranger station, travel east through town and turn right onto 15th street. Follow this road for about 15.5 miles to where the pavement ends, and continue on. In another 2.5 miles you come to a "Y" and you want to bear right. This is Forest Service Road 40. Continue for another 5 miles where you come to a junction with Forest Service Road 42. Continue on Forest Service Road 40 for 8 miles and take a right onto Forest Service Road 4030. Follow this road for .1 mile, and bear left at the "Y" and continue on for another .5 miles to the campground.

COMMENTS: This forested campground is set near a meadow, with views that are unbelievable. There are lots of trees for shade. As far as hiking, you could walk forever.

> *"The idea of wilderness needs no defense, it only needs defenders"*
>
> *~Edward Abbey*

WICKIUP

Number of sites: 5   Type: tents
Toilets: yes   Setting: forest; mountain
Tables: yes   Fire: fire grates
Fishing: yes   Hiking: yes
Handicap Access: no   Elevation: 5100 feet
          GPS: Lat: 46.13697   Long: -117.4354

DIRECTIONS: [GARFIELD] From the Pomeroy ranger station, travel east through town and turn right onto 15th street. Follow this road for about 15.5 miles to where the pavement ends, and continue on. In another 2.5 miles you come to a "Y" and you want to bear right. This is Forest Service Road 40. Continue for another 5 miles where you come to a junction with Forest Service Road 42. Continue on Forest Service Road 40 and in about 8.1 miles you'll come to a junction with Forest Service Roads 43 and 44. Stay straight on Forest Service Road 43 to the campground on your left.

COMMENTS: Located near the Triple Ridge area surrounded by the Jones, Huckleberry, and Hogback ridges; Wickiup Campground offers great hiking opportunities, within five miles, and views. Cold water springs are available 100 yards below the campground and fishing can be found at Ranger Creek within 5 miles.

GODMAN

Number of sites: 8
Toilets: yes
Tables: yes
Fishing: yes
Handicap Access: no

Type: tents
Setting: forest; creek
Fire: fire grates
Hiking: yes
Elevation: 6050 feet

GPS: Lat: 46.100143   Long: -117.786865

DIRECTIONS: [COLUMBIA] From the Pomeroy Ranger Station, travel west on Highway 12 for 3.9 miles and take a left onto the Tatman Mountain Road. Follow this road for 7 miles and bear right at the "Y". In just a bit the pavement ends. Continue on this gravel road for 2 miles where you'll come to a stop sign and a paved road. Turn left and follow this road for about 10.4 miles and turn right on the road signed for the Godman Ranger Cabin. Keep going and in 1.2 miles bear right at the "Y" and follow this road for 3 miles where you'll come to another "Y" and this time bear left. Continue on for another 11.7 miles to the campground on the right.

COMMENTS: How about those views on that last 11 mile stretch! Godman Campground has several secret treasures. There are numerous recreation opportunities available at this campground such as fishing, bicycling, and hiking. This campground location offers good views and great sunsets. The nearby Godman Trailhead provides access to West Butte Trail #3138 which enters Wenaha-Tucannon Wilderness.

SPRING LAKE CAMP   (DAYTON)

Number of sites: 8   Type: tents; small trailers
Toilets: yes   Setting: open area
Tables: yes (4)   Fire: fire grates
Fishing: yes   Hiking: yes
Handicap Access: no   Elevation: 2400 feet
                GPS: Lat: 46.33292   Long: -117.6761

DIRECTIONS: [COLUMBIA] From Dayton, travel east on Highway 12 for about 15 miles and take a right onto the Tucannon Road. Spring Lake Camp is about 25 miles down this road on the right side of the road and the first of ten WDFW camps on this road.

COMMENTS: This camp sets right off the road with some sites back on the hill. There was a fire here not long ago so don't expect much shade.
Discover Pass

BLUE LAKE CAMP   (DAYTON)

Number of sites: 12   Type: tents; small trailers
Toilets: yes   Setting: open area
Tables: yes (3)   Fire: fire grates
Fishing: yes   Hiking: yes
Handicap Access: no   Elevation: 2400 feet
            GPS: Lat: 46.324134   Long: -117.6700594

DIRECTIONS: From Dayton, travel east on Highway 12 for about 15 miles and take a right onto the Tucannon Road. Blue Lake Camp is about 1/4 mile past Spring Lake Camp on the right side of the road.

COMMENTS: Another camp that was burned, little shade here. Blue Lake is walking distance from camp on the same side of the road.
Discover Pass

RAINBOW LAKE CAMP (DAYTON)

Number of sites: 10
Toilets: yes
Tables: yes (2)
Fishing: yes
Handicap Access: no

Type: tents; small trailers
Setting: forest; lake
Fire: fire grates
Hiking: yes
Elevation: 2220 feet

GPS: Lat: 46.3141924 Long: -117.6587264

DIRECTIONS: From Dayton, travel east on Highway 12 for about 15 miles and take a right onto the Tucannon Road. Blue Lake Camp is about 1 mile past Blue Lake Camp on the left side of the road.

COMMENTS: After entering the site there is a fish hatchery. Continue straight to the campground entrance. There are some nice sites here, some right off the entrance road and some hidden back in the woods. The only two tables are located near the front of the campground. Nice campground. **Discover Pass**

DEER-WATSON CAMP (DAYTON)

Number of sites: 10
Toilets: yes
Tables: yes (4)
Fishing: yes
Handicap Access: no

Type: tents; small trailers
Setting: open area
Fire: fire grates
Hiking: yes
Elevation: 2230 feet

GPS: Lat: 46.3053841 Long: -117.6514035

DIRECTIONS: From Dayton, travel east on Highway 12 for about 15 miles and take a right onto the Tucannon Road. Deer-Watson camp is about 4.5 miles further on down the road from Rainbow Lake Camp and on the right side of the road.

COMMENTS: This is another camp set close to the road without much shade. The good is that the area you are in offers lots of hiking trails and much to explore. **Discover Pass**

WATERMAN CAMP   (DAYTON)

Number of sites: 7   Type: tents; small trailers
Toilets: yes   Setting: forest
Tables: yes (1)   Fire: fire grates
Fishing: yes   Hiking: yes
Handicap Access: no   Elevation: 2440 feet
                 GPS: Lat: Not Available

DIRECTIONS: From Dayton, travel east on Highway 12 for about 15 miles and take a right onto the Tucannon Road. Waterman Camp is about 1.5 miles past Deer-Watson and on the left side of the road.

COMMENTS: The sites here all set rather close together. There is some shade here and room for tents and small trailers. **Discover Pass**

NORTH AND SOUTH CAMP   (DAYTON)

Number of sites: 8   Type: tents; small trailers
Toilets: yes   Setting: forest
Tables: yes (1)   Fire: fire grates
Fishing: yes   Hiking: yes
Handicap Access: no   Elevation: 2470 feet
                 GPS: Lat: Not Available

DIRECTIONS: From Dayton, travel east on Highway 12 for about 15 miles and take a right onto the Tucannon Road. North and south camp is a little over .5 miles further on past Waterman Camp and also on the left side of the road.

COMMENTS: This camp is in two sections. On the right side you'll find 3 sites with toilet and no table. On the left side are 5 sites with toilet and one table. This camp sets a little further back from the road and there is more shade to be found here. **Discover Pass**

BIG FOUR LAKE CAMP   (DAYTON)

Number of sites: 2   Type: tents
Toilets: yes   Setting: open area
Tables: yes   Fire: fire grates
Fishing: yes   Hiking: yes
Handicap Access: no   Elevation: 2600 feet
         GPS: Lat: 46.26048 Long: -117.66857

DIRECTIONS: From Dayton, travel east on Highway 12 for about 15 miles and take a right onto the Tucannon Road. Big Four Lake Camp is about 1.5 miles further on past North and South Camp.

COMMENTS: This camp sets above the road, you may have to take a run at it, and the sites are set at either end of the camp with enough room so you're not on top of each other. **Discover Pass**

SCHOOL CANYON CAMP   (DAYTON)

Number of sites: 2   Type: tents
Toilets: yes   Setting: open area
Tables: yes   Fire: fire grates
Fishing: yes   Hiking: yes
Handicap Access: no   Elevation: 2800 feet
         GPS: Lat: Not Available

DIRECTIONS: From Dayton, travel east on Highway 12 for about 15 miles and take a right onto the Tucannon Road. School Canyon Camp is another 2 miles or so further on from Big Four Lake Camp.

COMMENTS: As with Big Four Lake, this camp sets above the road with room between sites. **Discover Pass**

PENJAB NORTH CAMP

Number of sites: 7
Toilets: yes
Tables: yes (2)
Fishing: yes
Handicap Access: no

Type: tents; trailers
Setting: forest; open area
Fire: fire grates
Hiking: yes
Elevation: 3100 feet

GPS: Lat: Not Available

DIRECTIONS: From Dayton, travel east on Highway 12 for about 15 miles and take a right onto the Tucannon Road. This camp is another 5 miles past the School Canyon Camp and on the right side of the road.

COMMENTS: This is a wide open camping area with enough room for tents, campers and trailers. **Discover Pass**

PENJAB SOUTH CAMP

(DAYTON)

Number of sites: 12
Toilets: yes
Tables: yes (2)
Fishing: yes
Handicap Access: no

Type: tents; trailers
Setting: forest; open area
Fire: fire grates
Hiking: yes
Elevation: 3200 feet

GPS: Lat: Not Available

DIRECTIONS: From Dayton, travel east on Highway 12 for about 15 miles and take a right onto the Tucannon Road. This camp is just up the road from Penjab North Camp.

COMMENTS: This is a rather large and open campground with vault toilet and 2 tables. The whole area offers much to do. There are rivers and creeks and a bunch of trails to explore. I hope you enjoy the area. **Discover Pass**

About the Author

Ray has lived in the State of Washington for the past 40 years and spends as much time as possible hiking and camping in this beautiful and remarkable Pacific Northwest. Now residing in the small town of Concrete he is the author of:

Ray's Guides: Free Campgrounds in Washington State,
Ray's Guides: Free Campgrounds in Oregon State,
Ray's Guides: Free Campgrounds in Idaho
Ray's Guides: Equestrian Camps in Washington & Oregon States

You can buy Ray's books online at:
www.raysguides.com
www.amazon.com

"Rivers, ponds, lakes and streams — they all have different names, but they all contain water. Just as religions do — they all contain truths."

~Muhammad Ali

Made in the USA
Middletown, DE
17 August 2016